$ 37.50

QUALITY INNOVATION

QUALITY INNOVATION

An Economic Analysis of
Rapid Improvements in
Microelectronic Components

G. M. P. SWANN

Q

Quorum Books
New York • Westport, Connecticut

338.476213817
S 97 q

Library of Congress Cataloging-in-Publication Data

Swann, G. M. P.
  Quality innovation.

  Based on the author's thesis (doctoral)—University
of London.
  Bibliography: p.
  Includes indexes.
  1. Microelectronics industry—Technological
innovations.   2. Integrated circuits industry—
Technological innovations.   3. Microelectronics.
4. Integrated circuits.   5. Competition.   I. Title.
HD9696.A2S9   1986   338.4'56213817   86-454
ISBN 0-89930-193-2 (lib. bdg. : alk. paper)

Published in the United States and Canada by
Quorum Books, Greenwood Press Inc., Westport, Connecticut

English language edition, except the United States and Canada,
published by Frances Pinter (Publishers) Limited

First published 1986

Library of Congress Catalog Card Number: 86-454

ISBN: 0-89930-193-2

Printed in the United States of America

The paper used in this book complies with the
Permanent Paper Standard issued by the National
Information Standards Organization (Z39.48-1984).

Typeset by Katerprint Co. Ltd Oxford

Contents

Foreword

This book stems from a lively doctoral thesis by Peter Swann that could have been published almost as it stood. Quality improvement is enabled by technical progress and driven by competition in a contest with no end and no eventual winner. The text books still incline to treat product differentiation as no more than a barrier to entry in stationary markets. Dr. Swann's approach is different. Its roots go back to Schumpeter rather than to Chamberlin. There are two sorts of innovation, both made possible by technological advance. First, there are new ways of satisfying old needs. A microchip displaces the bulb thermometer or the escapement of the watch. Second, there is the relentless incremental improvement of performance driven by competition, less dramatic but more pervasive.

This book deals in the main with the second kind. It sets up the framework for a theory of continuous product differentiation, combining several strands which have usually been separate. One strand is the theory of location (and clustering together) as applied to product-space. Another is the translation of quality edge ('vertical' differentiation) into its relative price equivalent. Another is the balance of technology-push and market-pull. Drawing all these together is the idea of 'supergame' playing in which powerful competitors are impelled to oust their own current products by the threat that rivals will forestall them.

Dr. Swann tests these ideas by tracing the dynamics of competition in microprocessors themselves. With their myriad of almost limitlessly refinable and recombinable components, there is no better practical example of that competitive quality improvement which drives so much industrial change.

Industrial economics has for a long time wandered in two of 'Error's fenny bogs and thorny brakes' (Rochester, 'Homo Sapiens'): namely the pursuit of equilibrium solutions and the abstract theory of games.

The prisoner's dilemma is central to competitive dynamics, as this book shows. But it is a dilemma without final resolution, played out, through product change, with luck for the wider benefit of society.

Professor D. K. Stout
11 November 1985

Acknowledgements

This book is a revised and shortened version of the author's doctoral thesis at the University of London. I am indebted to Tony Horsley for the most enjoyable and stimulating discussions on this research, and to Terence Gorman for all his advice at an early stage. In writing this book I have been helped and encouraged by a large number of people, too many to list here, but I would particularly like to thank the following: David Burningham, Martin Cave, Meghnad Desai, Walter Elkan, Peter Grindley, Richard Kaczynski, Bob Keyfitz, Steve Pudney, John Race, Richard Shaw, Peter Skott, David Stout, Dick Swann, Julia Swann, Hugh Wills. Finally, the late Alan Brown's encouragement was particularly valuable, and I am sorry he was not able to see the finished version.

I am grateful to the *Journal of Industrial Economics* for permission to reproduce material from a paper of mine (Volume 34, No. 1). Much of the research was carried out while I was at the International Centre for Economics and Related Disciplines at the London School of Economics, and I am most grateful to ICERD for financial support, and for providing a friendly atmosphere in which to work.

Appropriately perhaps, in view of the subject matter of the book, the various drafts of the book were typed by the author on a word-processor. Nevertheless, some of the early material was typed with great patience and accuracy by Ruth Singh, to whom I am most grateful.

My greatest debt is to my parents for their patient encouragement and understanding. To them this book is dedicated.

QUALITY INNOVATION

1 Introduction

'What do you do with a million components on a chip?'
Andrew Grove, President of Intel Corporation [1]

The quotation is a very succinct statement of the key issue addressed in this book. Rapidly expanding technological opportunities may tax the imagination of the firms trying to exploit them by quality innovation. Moreover, the immediate demand for improved qualities of products may not be particularly strong. Nevertheless, a process of vigorous innovation can continue. The history of developments in microelectronics from the 1960s to the present is an example of such a process at work.

Some explanation of the quotation is in order. A million components on a chip—that is, a digital integrated circuit containing a million transistors—represents an extraordinary technological opportunity. Intel Corporation have a reputation as the outstanding innovators in microelectronics during the 1970s, and they have not to date shown any inability to exploit technological opportunities. Nevertheless, the quotation can be read as, 'What do we (Intel Corporation) do with a million components on a chip?'

If the producer does not know what to do with a million components on a chip, the user knows even less. It has been said of some recently designed microprocessors that only a handful of programmers could immediately exploit the full potential of the devices. In due course, more users will be able to exploit this potential, and eventually such a level of quality may well become indispensable, though the emphasis must be on the word 'eventually'. Now the quotation can be read as, 'What do you (the user) do with a million components on a chip?'

Yet the process continues with vigour. The question is, 'What do you do?' rather than 'Do you do anything?' It may be that the majority of outstanding applications of microelectronics require no more than the existing technology, yet producers still indulge in vigorous quality innovation.

In short, then, our conclusion is this. The very rapid rates of quality innovation in microelectronic products do not necessarily imply that the immediate demand for improved quality products is particularly strong. The extraordinary rates of quality innovation in microelectronics cannot be fully understood without appreciating the competitive strategies adopted by firms to survive in this most competitive industry. Given the nature and potential of the technology, and the expectation that competitors will exploit this potential, firms are to some extent obliged to compete in rapid quality innovation. In summary, the market incentive for quality innovations may appear some time before the end-user is able to appreciate the true value of the innovation.

The title of this book may require a little clarification. By quality innovation we mean a particular form of product innovation: the introduction of a new (often improved) version of an existing product, rather than a completely new product. The quality innovation can be analyzed within an existing space of qualities or characteristics; the new product requires new dimensions.

This book attempts to do three things: first, to describe the history of quality innovation in microelectronics from the early 1960s to the mid-1980s; second, to interpret this history from the point of view of a theory of quality innovation; and third, to assess the effect of quality innovation on the demand for microelectronics. In terms of the quotation above, the book describes what manufacturers have done with 'a million components on a chip', why they have done what they have done, and how that has influenced the use of microelectronics.

The structure of the book

Chapter 2 presents a concise account of the theory of quality innovation and the theory of quality choice. The distinction between quality innovation and product innovation in general may appear to be blurred, but we shall argue in Chapter 2 that a useful distinction can be made. Briefly, the essential difference is that quality innovations can be analyzed within an existing space of qualities or characteristics, while other product innovations may require new dimensions; the difference is important because the new product and the quality innovation involve different risks and offer different rewards.

The incentive for quality innovation is that it will shift the firm's demand curve. There are two reinforcing effects: the expansion of market demand, and the improvement in competitive position. We try to assess the effect of quality innovation on market demand in Chapter 7 (an econometric analysis of quality choice) and in Chapter 8 (three case studies of the use of microelectronics). While it would be difficult to explain the growth in demand for microelectronics without reference to quality innovation, this is by no means the only contributory factor.

How does quality innovation affect a firm's competitive position? There are really two issues here: first, to what extent does any quality innovation strengthen a firm's market position before any retaliation; and second, to what extent do rivals react to any such innovation, and to what extent do such reactions offset the effect of the original innovation? The answer to the second issue depends on whether firms cluster in product space. The theory of product competition is discussed in Chapter 2, and some evidence is discussed in Chapter 6. In the process of product competition in microprocessors, some evidence of clustering is found; this would tend to reduce the competitive advantage obtained by quality innovation.

Chapter 3 describes the products that can be made with microelectronic technology, the measurement of computer systems and hence product quality, and the most important economic issues in the economics of production and product design. Microelectronic technology has been rich in technological opportunities over the period, even though large research and development expenditures are needed to realize these opportunities—as much as 10 per cent of sales revenue.

Chapter 4 describes in broad outline the history of quality innovation in microelectronics from the 1960s to the mid-1980s, while Chapters 5 and 6 look at particular aspects of that history in more detail.

Three features have been particularly striking about the developments in the technology. First, the rapid decline in prices of microelectronic components, probably unequalled by any other good. Second, the substantial and continuing improvements in product quality, especially in speed, reduced power consumption, reliability and capacity. Third, the continual appearance of new components, though some 'new' components can in fact be thought of as improved versions of old components, or as improved versions of collections of old components. Besides these developments in the technology, there has been a rapid growth in awareness of the technology, especially since 1975.

Chapter 5 shows how the quality innovation in microprocessors can be described by a time series of price functions. The estimation of a time series of price functions raises some quite interesting econometric issues. Moreover, it is a preliminary to the econometric analysis of quality choice. Broadly speaking, there is a downward trend in the prices of all microprocessors over the period, with the prices of higher quality products falling faster than the prices of lower quality products. While the price function is useful as a means of describing overall price movements, it is not so suitable for describing the strategy of quality innovation for individual firms.

Chapter 6 describes the quality innovation strategies of individual producers of microprocessors. There is evidence of clustering in product space, which suggests that the competitive advantage brought about by quality innovation is to some extent eroded. Nevertheless, it is argued that this clustering is probably an indication of important 'agglomeration' economies, or mutual economies accruing to firms producing similar products.

Chapter 7 examines the changing demand for microelectronics over the period. This is partly descriptive, and we observe that while sales of the high quality categories may grow relatively quickly, some of these still account for only a small proportion of total sales. In addition, we report the results of a preliminary attempt at quality demand analysis for different qualities of microprocessor. The data are too imperfect and the sample too short for the analysis to be more than exploratory. Nevertheless, the technique could be promising with more sympathetic data.

To give an alternative perspective to the analysis of quality demand, it was useful to carry out some case studies. Chapter 8 reports the results of three studies: the application of microelectronics in car engine control, telephone exchanges and electronic calculators. In each case, we try to assess from an engineering point of view whether the quality of available components has acted as a constraint on the development of that application. The most important thing about these case studies is that they give us a realistic perspective on the many issues that must be resolved before microelectronics can be used in a particular application. In two cases, quality innovation is not really crucial to the use of microelectronics, except perhaps in a very narrow sense; in the third, it is. This is, of course, only limited evidence, and we very briefly review some other case-study evidence.

Is it possible, then, to draw a broad generalization? Can we say for instance, that the spread in use has been constrained by the cost and quality of the available technology or, on the other hand, by the increase in awareness of the technology, and of how it may be exploited? It is not clear that there is one answer to this question which holds true throughout the 1960s, 1970s and 1980s. Barron and Curnow, writing in the late 1970s, suggest that the situation has changed in recent years. We quote them at some length here, for the passage sums up one rather prevalent line of argument (Barron and Curnow, 1979, pp. 45–6):

It would seem that, in the past, the development of computing has been limited to a considerable extent by the available technology. The creation of new applications and the opening of new markets has followed technological innovation, and the prediction of technological innovation has therefore been a good basis for predicting developments in the use of computing. The view is taken that this situation no longer pertains. With the latest developments in microelectronics, a vast reservoir of technology has been opened up and it will be a long while before this reservoir is fully exploited. Further advances in the technology are thought unlikely to have a substantial effect on the way information technology will develop in the medium to long term.

What, then, are the significant factors that will shape the way information technology develops? The most important, in our view, are the diffusion of knowledge about the technology and the social responses which the adoption of a pervasive technology will generate.

Chapter 9 draws together the main conclusions. Quality innovation is expensive and while one firm's innovation can increase its market share at the expense of rivals, the innovations of one firm to some extent cancel out those of another. Moreover, it is not certain that there are a large number of potential consumers for whom only the highest quality will suffice. Nevertheless, given the very considerable technological opportunity, and the expectation that rivals will try to exploit this opportunity, firms feel obliged to make use of rapid quality innovation.

Note

1. Quoted in *Electronics Industry*, August 1980, p. 3. The innovative record of Intel Corporation has been widely discussed: see, for example, 'Innovative Intel', *The Economist*, 16 June 1979, pp. 94–5.

2 The Theory of Quality Choice and Quality Innovation

The purpose of this chapter is to give an outline of the theory of quality choice and quality innovation. Both of these are large topics in their own right, and accordingly our attention will be confined to those parts of the theory of particular relevance to the study.

Much economic analysis of quality has made use of three techniques: the additive characteristics model, the idea of 'repackaging', and 'hedonic' analysis. These techniques have provided many useful insights but are not entirely satisfactory for the analysis in this study. Section 2.1 gives a brief review of these techniques, and their limitations.

Section 2.2 sets out the static theory of quality choice, as developed by Horsley(1983). Consumer choice depends on the price function, relating price to quality. To analyze the demand for a new improving durable good, however, the analysis must be extended in two ways. First, it is widely recognized that the growth in demand for a new good cannot be explained simply in terms of price reductions and quality improvements. Part of the growth in demand may be a result of 'pure diffusion' or competitive pressure to adopt: demand would grow as more users learn about the product and how to exploit it, even if price and quality did not change. Second, the purchase of a durable good can be postponed or brought forward to take advantage of price movements. Thus the user who would be prepared to buy at the existing price and quality may postpone purchase in anticipation of impending price reductions or quality improvements. Accordingly, Sections 2.3 and 2.4 extend the static model to take account of diffusion and expectations respectively.

Section 2.5 discusses some aspects of the theory of quality innovation: the emphasis is on analyzing the value of quality innovation to the innovating firm. This is seen to depend on the market demand for quality and also on the extent to which the firm can improve its competitive position by quality innovation. The latter in turn depends on the character of the product competition process; for this reason, Section 2.6 summarizes some of the main results in the theory of spatial and product competition.

2.1 Some techniques for the economic analysis of product quality

Traditional economic analysis has paid more attention to price than to product quality. This is not because quality was of no importance in economic affairs. In the Middle Ages, for example, Italian merchants shipped wool from England to Italy—at some cost—because English wool was the finest. So important was this trade that an early Italian handbook[1] contained an extensive list of the prices of different qualities of wool from different parts of England and Scotland—an early price function! In the seventeenth century, the French Mercantilist Colbert considered quality—not price—of greatest importance in trade, and this was the main reason for a formidable programme of state supervision and regimentation of industry (Cole, 1939, pp. 350–1; Clark, 1947, p. 71).

The relative neglect of quality in economic theory is probably a reflection of the conceptual difficulty of theorizing about product quality, and the empirical difficulty of measuring quality. Nevertheless, many economists have sought a theory of product quality. Marshall (1966), for example, made many references to quality, noting in particular that, 'with every step in his progress upwards', man requires not merely larger quantities of goods, but better qualities and greater variety.[2] Perhaps the first theoretical treatment was that of Chamberlin (1933) in the context of monopolistic competition, while Waugh's (1929) study of vegetable prices was an early empirical analysis of quality.

The traditional treatment of quality in economic theory is clearly described in Debreu's *Theory of Value* (1959, p. 2.4, his emphasis): '. . . a *commodity* is therefore defined by a specification of all its physical characteristics, of its availability date, and of its availability location. As soon as any one of these three factors changes, a *different* commodity results.' Variations in quality, then, require new goods. There can be no quality innovation unless extra goods—and so extra dimensions—are added to the analysis. Moreover, there is no distinction between quality innovation and new products.

Three techniques in the analysis of quality

Three well-known strands of analysis have given explicit attention to product quality. They are:

(1) the additive characteristics or components analaysis of Gorman (1956), Lancaster (1966, 1971), Ironmonger (1972), and others:
(2) the 'repackaging' technique of Fisher and Shell (1968), also mentioned in Theil (1952–53), which describes a product as a quantity multiplied by a scalar quality measure;
(3) the 'hedonic' technique of Griliches (1971), used to calculate quality-adjusted price indices, anticipated to some extent by A. T. Court (1939)—see also Waugh (1929) and Frisch (1934).

These techniques will be briefly discussed below. All assume that there are a certain number of characteristics or qualities which give a complete description of different versions of a particular product. Naturally, such an assumption is required for any analysis of quality choice and quality innovation—see Section 2.2. Quality innovation is defined as a product innovation that can be described within a given space of characteristics, while a new product involves new characteristics.

We shall see that these three strands all have one feature in common: they seem to suggest that the difference between quality innovation and price reductions is not necessarily of great economic significance. An improved quality of good may offer no more than a collection of existing goods. Indeed, the very expression 'quality-adjusted' seems to suggest that quality is a nuisance, which obscures the conventional price and quantity analysis.

For some purposes this feature may be acceptable, even desirable; in general, however, we would argue that both from the point of view of quality choice and from the point of view of quality innovation, this feature is somewhat unsatisfactory. One of the best examples in microelectronics is, quite simply, size. When miniaturization is important—in many control systems, instruments, microcomputers, watches, calculators. etc.—a new miniature component is not merely equivalent to a collection of old bulky components. Moreover, from the point of view of competitive strategy, quality innovation—indeed, product innovation in general—is seen as a means of avoiding price competition; the product innovation and the cost-reducing process innovation are rather different. A framework within which they are indistinguishable is to some extent missing the point.

We would emphasize that these observations are not intended as general criticism of these techniques; indeed, these techniques were designed for other purposes. For the analysis in this book, we consider that the techniques in Section 2.2 are more appropriate.

Additive characteristics or components

There are two particularly important assumptions in the original components or characteristics approach:

(1) Characteristics are additive in the sense that a combination of two goods with characteristics z_1 and z_2 is equivalent to a good with characteristics $z_1 + z_2$. This can be generalized to allow characteristics to be combined in slightly different ways—see Gorman (1976, p. 223–4).

(2) Consumer preferences are defined over characteristics aggregates, and not over the quantities of goods *per se*.

The additivity of characteristics can give rise to a number of difficulties,[3] but the most important in this context is that it may be possible to find a combination of lower quality goods that will be a match for (or better than) an improved quality good. If so, a higher quality good would offer no more than a combination of existing goods, except perhaps at a lower price.

Relaxing linear additivity in favour of other ways of combining characteristics might make for greater realism in the characteristics model, but the same feature remains. It is the result of a separability assumption which allows us to define an aggregate level of each characteristic, i.e. assumption (2) above.

This is not to say that the characteristics approach is inappropriate for all economic analysis; indeed, in computer system measurement, individual resources are combined to form a system aggregate. In the case of memory capacity, for example, component parts are clearly additive. Processing speed is in some cases additive, in the sense that two processors of a given speed can—by parallel processing—do the work of a processor of twice the speed. But that is about as far as it goes. When it comes to considerations such as miniaturization and low power consumption, which do not come into traditional computer system measurement, then additivity does not work.[4]

Repackaging

In the simple repackaging model of Fisher and Shell (1968), it is assumed that each good is quality adjusted—that is, it is the product of a quantity and a scalar-valued function of its qualities. Consumer preferences are defined over these quality-adjusted goods. Here the qualities of characteristics for any good must form a weakly separable group.

It is evident that quality improvements are simply equivalent to more of a good. Notice, too, that the quality multipliers used to calculate quality-adjusted quantities are the same functions as would be used to deflate prices in the calculation of quality-adjusted prices.

It might be added that while neither characteristics models nor repackaging are entirely satisfactory on their own, in combination they have drastic implications. The two forms of weak separability used above can be called overlapping, and they satisfy the conditions for Gorman's theorem (1968).[5] The result is that the two in combination imply additive separability over the elementary characteristics. This is quite unacceptable in general, and it is clearly essential to abandon one or other of these two separability assumptions.

Hedonic analysis

There is some ambiguity about the use of the term 'hedonic' in economics. In one sense, the term 'hedonic price function' is simply used to describe a function relating price to characteristics or quality. In this sense, it is no different from the price functions that will be discussed and estimated below (Sections 2.2–2.4 and Chapter 5); the use of such a function does not imply that quality innovation and price reductions are equivalent. In another sense, the term 'hedonic' is used to describe what is, in effect, a price deflator—a scalar measure of quality which, when divided into price, gives a quality-adjusted price. This scalar 'hedonic' measure is essentially the same idea as simple repackaging, as discussed above.

Thirdly, the term 'hedonic method' is used to describe attempts to derive consumer valuations of characteristics from estimated price functions. The question of whether a price function alone can identify consumers' preferences is an old one and it has generated a lot of confusion. Triplett (1975) presents a very simple explanation along the following lines.

Were all consumers identical and all producers identical, then simple considerations would suggest that only one quality of the good be produced. The observed variety of products suggests that there is a diversity of consumers or a diversity of producers, or both. If all consumers are identical, with identical real incomes, then each observed point in price/quality space is on the same consumer indifference curve. The price function identifies consumer preferences. If, on the other hand, all producers are identical and make identical profits, then each observed point lies on a producer constant profit contour. The price function identifies the profit function.

If, however, consumers and producers are diverse, then the price function represents an envelope of diverse indifference curves, and also an envelope of diverse profit functions. This envelope will not, in general, tell us very much about producer costs or consumer preferences.

Take any two points on a price function. There is no reason why any particular producer would make equal profits at those two points, so the price function alone will not identify any particular producer's profit function. Moreover, unless the producing industry is competitive, there is no reason why a firm that produces at one point should make the same profits as a firm producing at the other point. In general, then, the price function alone will not even identify a 'best-practice' profit function. Similar arguments apply to the consumption side. The final consumer can hardly be said to sell his output (utility) in a competitive market, nor are producers capable of first-degree price discrimination, so different consumers will enjoy different amounts of consumer surplus. Moreover, the idea of a best-practice consumption technology for a good with diverse uses is rather far-fetched.

In the competitive case, Rosen (1974) discusses the equilibrium determination of the price function. In the case where all consumers are identical, Muellbauer (1974) shows how the price function can be interpreted in either the characteristics context or the repackaging context, and derives the implications for consumer preferences.

2.2 The static analysis of quality choice

The analysis of quality choice is a straightforward generalization of the conventional analysis of demand. Instead of maximizing utility $u(x)$ with respect to several quantities (x is a vector), subject to the budget constraint $x'p \leq m$, the problem is to maximize $u(x.z)$ with respect to quantity x and quality z, subject to $xp(z) \leq m$, where $p(z)$ is a price function defined over quality z. The problem was first treated by L. M. Court (1941); the analysis here follows Horsley (1983).[6]

As L. M. Court was perhaps first to realize, the problem has inherently infinite dimensional aspects to it. Whereas in traditional demand analysis, there are a finite number of goods whose prices are defined by a finite dimensional vector, here there is a continuum of goods whose prices are defined by a price function—essentially an infinite dimensional vector. For the traditional case, Debreu partitioned commodity space into a finite number of intervals, whereas here no such partition is attempted. The infinite dimensional analysis of equilibrium is very difficult, but the generalization of demand analysis can be accomplished relatively easily, with only three additions to the economist's calculus armoury. These are the ideas of a functional, the functional derivative, and the point measure.

Quality choice: a simple exposition

We examine first the question of how the consumer chooses one quality from a wide range of qualities of a good. For the moment, we abstract from the question of what quantity of that particular quality to buy by assuming that he buys only one. The analysis here is informal; a formal statement will follow in the discussion of quality and quantity choice.

It is assumed that the range of qualities available to the consumer and their prices can be described by a price function. This price function is really no more than a price list giving the prices of goods of different qualities. We shall assume that the function is continuous and differentiable. This would be a fairly strong assumption if there were only a small range of qualities, for then the price list is not continuous or differentiable, and it is not defined over all points in the domain.[7] Nevertheless, much the same objections could be made to the idea of a smooth micro production function. A smooth function is just a convenient summary of the set of production techniques.

Figure 2.1 shows the price function $p(.)$ defined over one characteristic, z. The price function is only defined for qualities up to z_{max}; this is because z_{max} represents the highest available quality. Figure 2.1 also shows three consumer indifference curves between price and quality: u_1, u_2 and u_3. It is easiest to think of the indifference curve as a contour of the mixed direct/indirect utility function $v(m-p,z;r)$, where m is the budget and r is the price of other goods. The indifference curve u_i shows

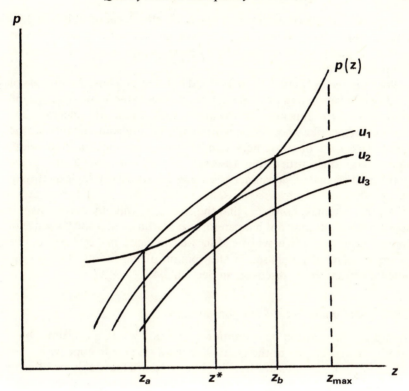

Figure 2.1   Quality choice

combinations of p and z for which:

$$v(m-p,z;r) = u_i$$

As drawn, the consumer has a diminishing marginal willingness to pay for quality while the price function shows an increasing marginal cost of quality.

Suppose that if he only buys other goods, the consumer can reach a level of utility u_1, but no higher. Then he will clearly benefit from buying any of the qualities between z_a and z_b; $v(m-p(z),z;r) \geq v(m;r)$ for any quality between z_a and z_b. As the indifference curves are drawn, the best choice is z^*, where the indifference curve u_2 is tangent to the price function. It would be easy to draw the indifference curves such that the best choice was a corner solution (z_{max}).

Naturally, if the consumer can reach a higher level of utility (u_3) by buying only other goods, then he will not buy any quality of this particular good—in this case, $v(m;r) \geq v(m-p(z),z;r)$, for any point on the price function.

We shall see in Section 2.5 below and in Chapter 5 how the process of quality innovation and price reductions increases the value of z_{max}, and shifts the price function downwards. Such shifts will increase the number of people who find it worthwhile buying some quality of the good. Two sorts of consumers stand to gain from such an innovation; first, a consumer with a low reservation price for any quality of the good, and second, a consumer requiring a particularly high quality of the good.

All this assumes, however, that the consumer will buy as soon as it is worthwhile. This may not happen for two reasons. First, the presence of 'pure' diffusion, which will be discussed in Section 2.3. Second, the postponement of purchases in anticipation of impending shifts in the price function; this is discussed in Section 2.4.

Quality and quantity choice: a formal exposition

Again we shall restrict our attention to the case where a consumer buys one particular quality of the good. The theory is able to cope with cases where several varieties are bought, but these will inevitably be difficult to handle in econometric work since they involve set-valued functions.

In the previous notation, the problem is to choose quality z and quantity x to maximize $u(x,z)$ subject to $xp(z) \leq m$. The quality z is taken to be a scalar in the discussion below, but the analysis is easily generalized to a vector of qualities. Assuming that all the budget is spent, the corresponding Lagrangean is:

$$\max u(x,z) + \lambda(m-xp(z))$$

At the optimum (x^*,z^*,λ^*), the first order conditions are:

$$u_x(x^*,z^*) = \lambda^*p(z^*)$$
$$u_z(x^*,z^*) = \lambda^*x^*p'(z^*)$$
$$m = x^*p(z^*) \tag{2.1}$$

For an interior solution, the optimization problem is demonstrated graphically in Figure 2.2. This is rather more familiar than Figure 2.1 showing conventionally-shaped indifference curves and a budget set—

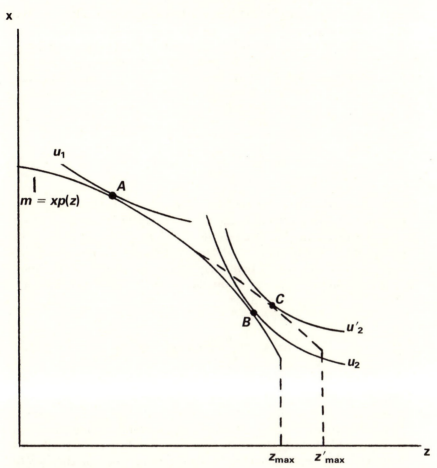

Figure 2.2 Quality and quantity choice

the area under the line $m = xp(z)$. The budget set stops at the quality z_{max}; this is because z_{max} is the highest quality available.

The figure gives a clear indication of how a change in the budget set will affect quality and quantity choice. Suppose, for example, that the prices of the highest quality goods fall a little, so that the budget set shifts out to the broken line at the high quality end. The consumer with indifference curve u_1 is not affected by this price change, and remains at point A. On the other hand, the consumer with indifference curve u_2 buys more of a higher quality good; that is, he moves from B to C. The essential point is that the budget set has changed its shape in the neighbourhood of point B, but not in the neighbourhood of point A.

The argument can be formalized. Optimum quality choice (and quantity choice) is a functional of the price function, defined by equations (2.1). Following Horsley (1983), we can use Volterra's functional derivative to derive the effect of a small adjustment to the price function. This effect is given by the total differential:

$$\delta z^* = \int_0^{z_{max}} \frac{\delta z^*}{\delta p(z)} \, \delta p(z) \, dz \tag{2.2}$$

where $\delta z^*/\delta p(z)$ is the functional derivative, giving the effect on quality choice of a small adjustment to the price function at quality z. If, as we argued above, quality choice z^* is only disturbed by changes in the price function at z^*, then the functional derivative is zero, except at the point $z = z^*$. In that case, we say that the quality choice functional (equation 2.1) is 'specially dependent' upon the point (x^*, z^*), and the total differential (2.2) can be written:

$$\delta z^* = \int_0^{z_{max}} \frac{\delta z^*}{\delta p(z)} \, \varepsilon_{z^*} \, \delta p(z) \, dz \tag{2.3}$$

where ε_{z^*} is the point measure of unit mass at z^*, and zero mass elsewhere.

We can calculate the effect of a small adjustment to the price function on quality and quantity choice by expanding the first order conditions about the initial optimum (x^*, z^*). If the price function changes to $p + \Delta p$, and the budget to $m + \Delta m$, then at the new optimum (dropping some terms of second order):

$$u_x(x^* + \Delta x^*, z^* + \Delta z^*) = (\lambda^* + \Delta \lambda^*)(p(z^* + \Delta z^*) + \Delta p(z^*))$$
$$u_z(x^* + \Delta x^*, z^* + \Delta z^*) = (\lambda^* + \Delta \lambda^*)(x^* + \Delta x^*)(p'(z^* + \Delta z^*) + \Delta p'(z^*))$$
$$m + \Delta m = (x^* + \Delta x^*)(p(z^* + \Delta z^*) + \Delta p(z^*)) \tag{2.4}$$

Using Taylor's Theorem to expand this to terms of first order, and subtracting the result in (2.1), we obtain:

$$\begin{bmatrix} u_{xx} & u_{xz} - \lambda^* p'(z^*) & -p(z^*) \\ u_{zx} - \lambda^* p'(z^*) & u_{zz} - \lambda^* x^* p''(z^*) & -x^* p'(z^*) \\ -p(z^*) & -x^* p'(z^*) & 0 \end{bmatrix} \begin{bmatrix} \Delta x^* \\ \Delta z^* \\ \Delta \lambda^* \end{bmatrix} = \begin{bmatrix} \lambda^* \Delta p(z^*) \\ \lambda^* x^* \Delta p'(z^*) \\ x^* \Delta p(z^*) - \Delta m \end{bmatrix}$$

After inversion,[8] this yields the following differential demand equations for quality and quantity choice (the notation should be self-explanatory):

$$\begin{bmatrix} \Delta x^* \\ \Delta z^* \\ \Delta \lambda^* \end{bmatrix} = \begin{bmatrix} B_{xx} & B_{xz} & B_p \\ B_{zx} & B_{zz} & B_{p'} \\ B_p & B_{p'} & B_m \end{bmatrix} \begin{bmatrix} \Delta p(z^*) \\ x^* \Delta p'(z^*) \\ (x^* \Delta p(z^*) - \Delta m)/\lambda^* \end{bmatrix} \qquad (2.5)$$

These differential demand equations are comparable to the Rotterdam Model of Theil (1965) and Barten (1969).[9] The special dependence of these demand equations on local adjustments to the price function is of great econometric significance, and represents a considerable saving in terms of parameters. It is important to notice that the demand equations give the changes in quantity and quality that result from a change in the price function; this must not be confused with a change in price paid resulting from the consumer's choice to consume a different quality.

Quality demand analysis with aggregate data

The differential demand equations (2.5) would be ideal if we had data on the quality and quantity purchases of individual consumers. The demand analysis of Chapter 7, however, has to make do with aggregate sales of seven qualities of microprocessor. Aggregation is a well-known problem in demand analysis, but it is usually argued that there is no difficulty in constructing a price aggregate, since all consumers face the same prices.

Unfortunately, this argument does not hold here. That may be surprising, since we can certainly assume that all consumers face the same price function. Nevertheless, it is apparent from the first order conditions (2.1) that the 'price' of quality ($x^* p'(z^*)$) depends on the quantity bought: consumers buying different quantities will face different prices for quality. If, however, we assume that all consumers buy the same fixed quantity—so that consumers have only to choose quality—then there is no aggregation problem with prices. Moreover, aggregate demand—like individual demands—shows the same 'special dependence' on local adjustments to the price function.

For any given price function, let us define an aggregate sales function, $F(.)$, such that $F(z)$ gives the aggregate sales of quality z. Then $F(.)$ is given by:

$$F(\bar{z}) = \int_{\theta} x^*(\theta) \, \varepsilon_{z^*(\theta)} \, \varepsilon_{\bar{z}} f(\theta) \, d\theta \qquad (2.6)$$

Where θ acts as an index to the different consumers, $x^*(\theta)$ and $z^*(\theta)$ represent the quantity and quality choices of consumers of type θ, $f(\theta)$ is a density function, giving the density of consumers of type θ, $\varepsilon_{z^*(\theta)}$ is a point measure of unit mass at $z^*(\theta)$, and $\varepsilon_{\bar{z}}$ is a point measure of unit mass at $\bar{z}$.

The value of $F(z_0)$, for example, is obtained by sorting out all the consumers who buy quality z_0 (the point measure does this sorting) and then adding up their individual purchases. As we saw above, the different consumers buying quality z_0 will not necessarily have the same 'prices' for quality. Then the aggregate demand for quality z_0 will depend on a range of prices for quality.

If, however, we could assume that all consumers buy the same fixed quantity, then all consumers buying z_0 would face the same price for quality. Then the aggregate demand for quality z_0 would depend on only one price for quality. Moreover, since the individual demand functions are specially dependent on local adjustments to the price function, then the aggregate demand for a particular quality z_0 would be specially dependent on changes in the price function at z_0.

2.3 Dynamics of demand: 'pure' diffusion

The model of quality and quantity choice discussed in the last section is a static model. An exercise in comparative statics yielded demand equations (2.5) which could in principle be used to analyze the way in which demand changes over time. Indeed, with a well-established good, the model could be used without modification. The model could, however, give misleading results if it were applied without modification to the demand for a new good. The problem is this. It would be misleading to attribute all the growth in demand to changes in the price function (and income). It is well recognized that some of the growth in demand for a new good arises firstly because more potential consumers learn about the product and how to use it, and secondly because of an increasing competitive pressure to use it.

This is important for three reasons. Firstly, the unmodified static model might give misleading results. Secondly, consumer awareness and understanding is hard to measure. Thirdly, there is some uncertainty about the way in which awareness and understanding diffuses through the economy.

Diffusion and 'pure' diffusion[10]

The term diffusion is used to describe the growth in demand for a new good, or a new technology. Many writers use the term in a very broad sense: growth in demand is diffusion irrespective of how that growth comes about.

In principle, however, it would be interesting to distinguish at least four possible influences at work here:

(1) A growing number of people learn about the good or technology and how to make use of it.

(2) The profitability of adopting a new technology can change over time; similarly, the competitive pressure to adopt will increase as more and more competitors start to use the innovation.

(3) The real price of the good may fall over time and the quality may increase; this would make it attractive to a larger proportion of potential buyers.

(4) Over a longer horizon or even within a business cycle, changes in income or profits can influence the decision to buy.

All four of these influences contribute to diffusion; we reserve the term 'pure' diffusion for the first influence, while accepting that in some cases it may be hard to distinguish (1) from (2).

Epidemic models of 'pure' diffusion

The best-known model of 'pure' diffusion is the so-called epidemic model. In its simplest form, the model contains no economic influences as such. It is assumed that the price and quality of the good are sufficiently attractive from the beginning that all consumers would buy if they knew of the good's existence. Diffusion, then, is simply a matter of how fast people learn. The diffusion process that results is thought to be rather like the spread of an infectious disease—without, necessarily, any pejorative implications.

Each member of the population is assumed to have equal susceptibility to the disease, and their susceptibility does not change over time. People circulate at random and make one contact in a short time-interval. If a healthy person meets someone with the disease, there is a fixed probability (π) that the healthy person will catch the disease. In the short interval, the number who catch the disease will be the number of healthy people, times the probability that they meet an unhealthy person, times the probability of contracting the disease on this meeting. That is:

$$\frac{dn}{dt} = \pi(N - n)\frac{n}{N} \qquad (2.7)$$

where N is the total number of people and n is the number of unhealthy people. This differential equation solves to give a logistic growth curve:

$$n = \frac{N}{1 + e^{-\pi(t - t^*)}} \qquad (2.8)$$

where t^* is the date at which the diffusion process is half complete. It is easiest to check this result in reverse. Differentiating (2.8), using the quotient rule, we obtain:

$$\frac{dn}{dt} = \frac{\pi N e^{-\pi(t - t^*)}}{[1 + e^{-\pi(t - t^*)}]^2}$$

Again using (2.8), this can be rewritten:

$$\frac{dn}{dt} = \frac{\pi N(N - n)/n}{(N/n)^2}$$

which is easily rearranged to give (2.7).

The logistic growth curve is very similar to a cumulative normal curve, and is symmetric about the point ($n = N/2$, $t = t^*$). Indeed, the symmetry of the growth curve can easily be seen from equation (2.7). For example, the slope of the growth curve is the same when a quarter are unhealthy as when three-quarters are unhealthy: if $n = N/4$, then $dn/dt = \pi 3N/16$; if $n = 3N/4$, then dn/dt is also equal to $\pi 3N/16$.

It would be wrong, however, to assume that this symmetry is an intrinsic property of all epidemic models. It is easy enough to construct variants which give rise to a negatively skewed growth curve. The symmetry of the traditional model depends, for example, on the assumption that the probability of a (to date) healthy person contracting the disease in any interval is independent of his previous exposure to the disease.

Simple considerations suggest that this is an unrealistic assumption to make when modelling the diffusion of information. When subjected to a lot of noise, people may be unable to sort out the good ideas from the bad. They do, however, have a reasonable short-term memory, so that if the same idea appears in a few successive intervals, it will merit special consideration. As a simple example, let us suppose that there is a small probability π_1 of 'catching the disease' if exposed to an 'unhealthy' person for one period at a time, but a higher probability π_2 if exposed to an 'unhealthy' person for two or more successive periods. Then following the same argument as used to obtain (2.7), we find that in any short time-interval the number 'contracting the disease' is:

$$\frac{dn}{dt} = (N - n)\left[\pi_1 \frac{n}{N} \frac{(N-n)}{N} + \pi_2 \left(\frac{n}{N}\right)^2\right] \tag{2.9}$$

If $\pi_1 < \pi_2$, then the probability of any healthy individual contracting is no longer simply proportional to the unhealthy fraction of the population, but is a quadratic function of the unhealthy fraction. This is easily seen by rearranging (2.9) to obtain:

$$\frac{dn}{dt} = (N - n)\left[\pi_1 \frac{n}{N} + (\pi_2 - \pi_1) \left(\frac{n}{N}\right)^2\right] \tag{2.10}$$

In this case, a negatively skewed growth curve will be the result. When $n/N = 1/4$, for example, the slope of the growth curve is $(3\pi_1 + \pi_2)3N/64$; if $n/N = 3/4$, however, the slope is $(\pi_1 + 3\pi_2)3N/64$. The growth of demand is relatively rapid as the market becomes saturated.

Many models of this sort could be constructed, but for the purpose of this study the main point is this: it would be wrong to presume that this purely epidemic type of diffusion implies a symmetric growth curve.

The analysis of quality and quantity choice with pure diffusion

In the light of all this, how can we use the static model of quality and quantity choice to analyze the demand for a new product? If we have data on the quality and quantity purchases of individual consumers at different dates, we might argue that these data can be analyzed without paying any attention to pure diffusion: the consumer is 'infected' at all dates. On the other hand, there could be degrees of understanding and awareness; to put it another way, consumer tastes are not constant at all dates.

If, however, we only have aggregate data on the growth of total purchases of different qualities, then we cannot ignore pure diffusion. As mentioned above, awareness is difficult to measure, and we saw that there is some uncertainty about the rate at which awareness diffuses to potential consumers. A crude allowance for pure diffusion is to introduce a time trend into the equation for aggregate purchases of a particular quality. An equivalent procedure for differential demand equations such as (2.5) is to introduce a constant term. Nevertheless, there is some uncertainty about the appropriate shape of the time trend. Ideally it should be the same shape as the pure diffusion growth curve, but we do not know the exact shape of this growth curve. It might be thought that this hardly matters, and that any approximation will do. We shall see in Chapter 7, however, that regressions with several collinear regressors make considerable demands on data accuracy.

If instead of examining aggregate purchases of particular qualities we look at shares of aggregate expenditure on all qualities of the good, we might argue that to a first order of approximation, pure diffusion can be ignored. Suppose, for example, that the price function was the same at two different dates, but that because of pure diffusion, total purchases at the later date were much larger than at the earlier date. Then, so long as the sets of consumers at the two dates both represent random samples from the same population, then the expected distribution of expenditures between different qualities should be the same at the two dates. Then the expected effect of pure diffusion on the shares of aggregate expenditure would be zero, and in some sense pure diffusion could be ignored.

The problem with this last argument is that it may not be sensible to treat the two sets of consumers as random samples. A sample from a population is only generated by a random sampling procedure if all possible samples of that size have equal probability of being drawn: this is hardly true of the samples generated by pure diffusion.

In short, then, the effects of pure diffusion cannot really be ignored in the analysis of demand for a new good, and at the same time it is difficult to model pure diffusion explicitly. From this point of view, pure diffusion is a nuisance and complicates the demand analysis. Ironically, pure diffusion may sometimes serve to simplify the demand analysis. When consumers postpone purchases in expectation of impending price reductions, the analysis of demand is a little complicated. If the timing of purchases is a matter of pure diffusion alone, then the expectations effect does not come into play.[11]

Quasi Engel curves

Bonus (1973) tried to separate the effects of pure diffusion and income growth on the growth in demand for some consumer durables. To do this, he made use of the rather ingenious technique of plotting quasi Engel curves for different years;[12] this allowed him to distinguish the influence of income on demand from pure diffusion. (Bonus refers to the growth in the number of informed consumers as 'vertical' diffusion.) These quasi Engel curves give the proportion of consumers in a certain income bracket who own the good in question. Naturally, as Bonus himself observes, this procedure is open to the objections that cross-section income elasticities are not the same as time-series elasticities, and that in such a cross-section family composition differences should be taken into account. Moreover, the part which is attributed to vertical diffusion could, as Bonus again observes, be the result of price changes, quality changes, and so on.

In any case, such a procedure is not easily available for distinguishing the price and quality influences from vertical diffusion; after all, it is usually assumed that the price function does not vary in a cross-section. Prices and qualities do vary between countries in a cross-section, but then all sorts of other confusing forces come into play.

2.4 Dynamics of demand: expectations

It was argued above that the purchase of a durable good can be postponed or brought forward to take advantage of price movements. Thus a consumer who might be prepared to buy, given the existing price function, may still find it profitable to postpone purchase in anticipation of impending price reductions or quality improvements. Users of micro-electronics have come to expect a continuing process of quality innovation and price reductions. For that reason, the appropriate model with which to analyze the demand for a durable good of this sort should refer to the expected intertemporal price function.

How do consumers form expectations about quality improvements and price reductions? In the particular context of microelectronics, we shall return to this question in Chapters 3 and 4. In general, it may be that consumers make use of concepts such as the product life cycle and the learning curve.

Quality choice and timing

We present here a simple model of demand for a durable good:[13] in particular, the model analyzes quality choice and the timing of purchase. The analysis is similar to that in Section 2.2, and we again assume that the consumer buys only one particular quality. For simplicity we assume that the durable good cannot be resold,[14] and that the consumer buys a quantity of one.

The problem is to choose quality z and timing t to maximize the intertemporal utility function $u(z, t)$ subject to the constraint $p(z, t) \leq me^{rt}$, where $p(.,.)$ is the (expected) intertemporal price function, m is the budget available at time $t = 0$, and r is the discount rate. The budget constraint is a little unusual: it simply shows that if purchase is postponed from time $t = 0$ to time $t = t^*$, then the budget will grow from m to me^{rt^*}. Assuming that all the budget is spent, the Lagrangean is:

$$\max u(z,t) + \lambda(me^{rt} - p(z, t))$$

At the optimum (z^*, t^*, λ^*), the first order conditions are:

$$u_z(z^*, t^*) = \lambda^* p_z(z^*, t^*)$$
$$u_t(z^*, t^*) = \lambda^* [p_t(z^*, t^*) - rme^{rt^*}]$$
$$me^{rt^*} = p(z^*, t^*) \tag{2.11}$$

For an interior solution, the problem is shown graphically in Figure 2.3. The figure shows two indifference curves, and the expected budget set: the area below and to the right of the line $p = me^{rt}$. The figure makes it clear why the consumer may postpone purchase in anticipation of price reductions and quality innovation. Suppose instead that the consumer foresaw no further quality improvements, and expected prices to rise at the discount rate. Then the expected budget line would be a horizontal line to the right of the point $(z = z_0, t = 0)$. Then the optimum solution would be to buy quality z_0 at time 0. As it is, the consumer delays purchase until time t_1, when he buys a higher quality (z_1), and reaches a higher level of utility (u_1).

As they are drawn, the indifference curves exhibit minimum quality requirements, maximum waiting times, and a diminishing marginal willingness to wait for quality improvements: such properties seem sensible enough. As drawn, the budget line is upward-sloping and concave to the origin. The slope of the budget line is given by:

$$\frac{dz}{dt} = \frac{rp(z, t) - p_t(z, t)}{p_z(z, t)} \tag{2.12}$$

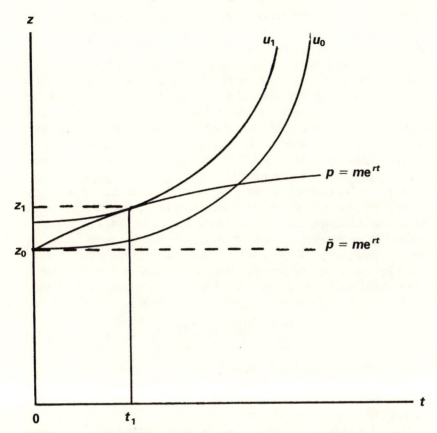

Figure 2.3 Quality choice and timing

Since the price of quality (p_z) is positive, this slope is clearly positive so long as the expected rate of inflation in the particular good is less than the discount rate: $p_t/p \leqslant r$. On the other hand, the budget line need not be concave to the origin. Using the quotient rule to differentiate (2.12) with respect to t, we obtain the second derivative of the budget line:

$$\frac{\mathrm{d}^2 z}{\mathrm{d} t^2} = \frac{p_z(rp_t - p_{tt}) - p_{zt}(rp - p_t)}{(p_z)^2} \tag{2.13}$$

The denominator is obviously positive, but the numerator could be positive or negative. The terms p_z, p and r are positive, while p_t is negative. The expression $rp - p_t$ is the numerator of the RHS of (2.12), and we argued that it would be positive. The term p_{zt} is negative if, as seems plausible, the marginal price of quality is expected to fall over time; if prices are falling, the term p_{tt} must become positive at some point, or prices would fall below zero.

Nevertheless, while we can put signs on all the terms in (2.13), all we can say is that the numerator is the difference between two negative terms. The second derivative of the budget line may be negative or positive, and accordingly the budget line may or may not be concave from below. It is not essential that the budget line is concave in this way, so long as it is tangent to the indifference curve from below; if it were tangent from above, then the first order conditions would of course correspond to a utility minimum!

While we cannot say anything in general about the shape of the budget line, we may observe that according to (2.12), the slope of the budget line is simply the ratio of the discounted expected rate of price reduction, $r - d\ln p/dt$, to the percentage premium for quality, $d\ln p/dz$. In Chapter 3, we shall see that these two quantities are closely related for microelectronic components. By making some reasonable assumptions about mark-up pricing, it is possible to show that for the typical qualities of microelectronic components that would be sold at any time:

$$\frac{d\ln z}{dt} \simeq \frac{d\ln g}{dt} - \frac{2}{3}\frac{d\ln f}{dt} + \frac{r}{3} \tag{2.14}$$

where: g represents gates per unit area of silicon, a measure of density or miniaturization; and f represents the mean number of faults per unit area of processed silicon, a measure of the quality of the production process.

The proof of this assertion requires some understanding of the nature of production costs in microelectronics, and is left to Chapter 3. Nevertheless, its simplicity is apparent: the shape of the budget line simply reflects the rate of progress of the technology parameters.

If the growth rate of g and the rate of decline of f are constant—and for much of the period 1960–80 they were—the solution to (2.14) is a budget line showing exponential growth in z. Such a budget line is clearly not concave to the origin, and could give rise to very curious results. As we shall see in Chapter 3, however, there are fundamental limits to the potential of the technology, and at some point the growth rate of g (and possibly the rate of decline of f) must tail off. For microelectronics, therefore, the choice of quality and timing is represented in Figure 2.4.

Figure 2.4 shows an indifference curve tangent to the non-concave

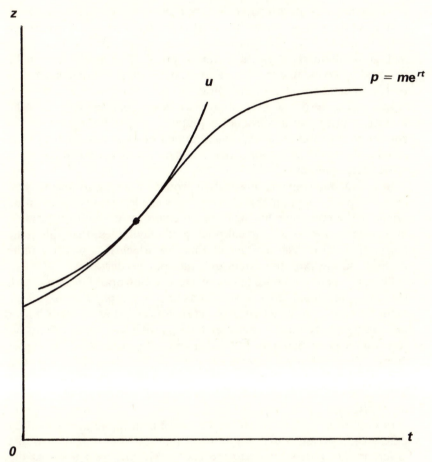

Figure 2.4 The intertemporal budget constraint for microelectronic components

part of the budget line. When indifference curves so nearly coincide with the budget line, it is apparent that small changes in either can lead to large changes in behaviour.

Reservation prices

In an illustrative example in Section 2.2, it was assumed that people would buy a good as soon as their reservation price was met. As remarked, however, this does not seem a very satisfactory assumption.

A consumer may be prepared to pay a price p_1 now for a particular good, but he may not actually buy at a price p_1 now if he expects the price to fall to p_2 in the near future. This suggests that there is some ambiguity about the term 'reservation price'. This ambiguity can be resolved by saying that the price a consumer is prepared to pay depends on his expectations about future prices.

In a static sense,[15] a reservation price has a clear meaning. It is the maximum price that a consumer is prepared to pay for a good. If this consumer were put in an experimental and timeless environment, and faced with a series of random prices, then his responses would reveal his static reservation price.

In a dynamic context, however, it would be wrong to assume that the price paid at first purchase will be the same as the static reservation price. If the consumer has delayed purchase in (correct) expectation of a price reduction, the actual price paid may be less than this static reservation price. The amount of time for which it is worth waiting depends on the expected extent of future price reductions.

Perhaps, then, it is useful to talk of a reservation price function, which gives the maximum price that a consumer is prepared to pay as a function of the expected path of future prices. Then it is no longer misleading to say that a consumer buys as soon as a price falls to his reservation price function. For if, after taking account of his expectations, the consumer is prepared to pay a price p_1, and the actual price is p_1, then he will buy. The conventional or static reservation price is simply this function evaluated when prices are not expected to change in the future.

In empirical analysis, it would be convenient if the prices paid by different consumers, buying at different times, told us something of the different values they attach to the good. Trivially, we know that the price each consumer pays when he buys reveals his reservation price function evaluated at the expectations he holds when he buys. Moreover, we know that, before he bought, his reservation price function evaluated at the expectations he held at that time lay below the market price. Beyond that we cannot say much. Take two consumers who buy at the same time. Unless we assume that they have the same expectations and same discount rate, we cannot say that their reservation price functions (evaluated at those like expectations) are equal. Even if we make that assumption, we cannot say anything about their reservation price functions when evaluated at other expectations.

Now consider two consumers who buy at different times. If we are to deduce relative static reservation prices from relative prices paid, then we must assume equal discount rates and similar expectations—'similar' in the sense that A, buying at time t_a, expects (at t_a) prices to follow the path, $p = f(t-t_a)$, and B, buying at time t_b, expects (at t_b) prices to follow the path, $p = f(t-t_b)$, where $f(.)$ is the same function in both cases, and $f(0) = 1$.

A simple example should help to make this clear. Suppose that a consumer buys a good to fulfil some project which yields an income stream of $y(t)$. If the project is started at time t, let $v(t)$ denote its value at time t (in terms of the discounted income stream after time t). For simplicity, assume that the income stream falls exponentially over time; that is, $y(t) = y(0)e^{-ht}$. Then it is readily apparent that the value also falls exponentially, since:

$$v(t) = \int_0^\infty y(t+s)\, e^{-rs}\, ds = y(0)\, e^{-ht} \int_0^\infty e^{-(h+r)s}\, ds$$

$$= \frac{y(0)}{h+r}\, e^{-ht} = v(0)\, e^{-ht}$$

where $v(0)$ is defined in an obvious manner.

The consumer expects at time $t = 0$ that the price of the good will fall from its current level of $p(0)$ at an exponential rate, $p(t) = p(0)e^{-qt}$. Clearly, then, the consumer withing to maximize present value should buy at that time which maximizes discounted profit:

$$(v(t) - p(t))e^{-rt} = v(0)e^{-(h+r)t} - p(0)e^{-(q+r)t}$$

where r is the discount rate. This gives the first order condition:

$$[-(h + r)v(t) + (q + r)p(t)]e^{-rt} = 0 \tag{2.15}$$

This can be solved to obtain t, but first notice that if $p(t) = v(t)(h + r)/(q + r)$, then the consumer should buy at time t. It should then be clear that the reservation price function is simply:

$$R(t) = v(t)(h + r)/(q + r) \tag{2.16}$$

To satisfy the second order condition for a maximum,[16] it is necessary that $q > h$, so that $R(t) < v(t)$.

The reservation price function depends on the discount rate, the project decay rate, and the expected decline in prices. If different consumers buying at different times have equal discount and project decay rates, and if they have the same expectation about the value of q, then the different prices paid do reveal their relative static reservation prices. If any one of these conditions does not hold, however, the prices paid do not reveal their relative static reservation prices.

From equation (2.15) it is easy to solve for t^* the optimum time of purchase. Gathering terms in t, we obtain:

$$e^{(g-h)t} = \frac{p(0)(q+r)}{v(0)(h+r)}$$

whence:

$$t^* = \frac{\ln[p(0)/v(0)] + \ln[(q+r)/(v+r)]}{q-h} \tag{2.17}$$

Figure 2.5 shows how t^* depends on q for various values of $p(0)/v(0)$. The example assumes a discount rate of $r = 0.1$, and for simplicity the income stream from this project does not decline over time ($h = 0$). The figure is interesting as it shows how, for low values of q, timing is very sensitive to small changes in q and $p(0)/v(0)$. The essential point is that when q is close to h, the indifference curve and the budget constraint very nearly coincide, and thus—as we saw before—timing is very sensitive to small changes in the budget constraint.

2.5 The theory of quality innovation

The three preceding sections have been concerned with quality choice from the point of view of the consumer. The last two sections in this chapter are concerned with quality innovation from the point of view of the producer. Corresponding to the theory of quality choice for a price-taking consumer, there is a competitive theory of quality choice for a price-taking producer. The producer chooses the design which maximizes his profits: for a given level of output, this is the design which maximizes the difference between the market price for that quality, and his production costs. Of course, since this is a competitive producer, his 'maximum' profits will be only 'normal' profits.

We do not pursue this competitive theory any further here, for two reasons. First, the character of this theory is very similar to the theory of consumer choice, which has already been set out in some detail. Second, and much more important, we take a Schumpeterian view of innovation

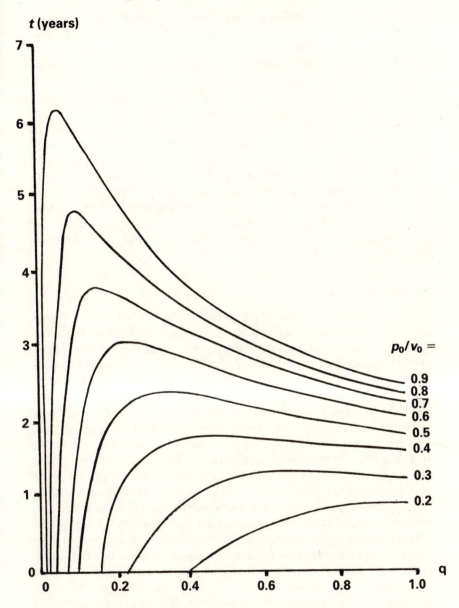

Figure 2.5 Timing of purchases

in this study. We argue that a competitive model of this sort does not capture the true incentive for innovation, which is to establish a (temporary and perhaps only weak) monopoly position. For this reason, we shall discuss quality innovation in an oligopolistic setting, where firms choose quality and price.

We note that there is a very substantial and wide-ranging literature which discusses the comparative incentive to innovate under different market structures, different licensing rules and varying degrees of uncertainty, and whether the resulting innovation is insufficient, optimal or excessive from a social efficiency point of view. Excellent reviews are available in Kamien and Schwartz (1982) and Dasgupta (1982). While the following discussion draws on various themes in this literature, there is only a limited overlap. This is because our primary concern is rather narrow, namely, to present a framework with which to evaluate the comparative value to the innovating firm of different sorts of quality innovation.

Types of product innovation

For the purposes of this study, we make a distinction between two types of product innovation. Quality innovation represents improved qualities of existing goods, and the quality innovation can be described within an existing space of characteristics or qualities. The new product, on the other hand, embodies new characteristics. The distinction may appear blurred: some of the more recent 16- and 32-bit microprocessors are certainly 'improved qualities of existing goods', but they undoubtedly embody 'new characteristics'. The distinction is useful, however, for two reasons. First, the effect of quality innovation on demand can be analyzed with the models of quality choice set out in Sections 2.2 and 2.4, while the effect of the new product cannot. Second, because the new product represents a more radical product innovation than the quality innovation, it offers a greater potential reward but involves a greater degree of market uncertainty (see Freeman, 1982, Chapter 7).

It is illuminating to compare the two from a Schumpeterian perspective. Non-price competition is seen not only as a means of establishing a decisive advantage over rivals, but also as a means of avoiding price competition which is seen as a particularly unstable process. Thus advertising, by establishing brand loyalties, discourages the consumer from comparing products on the basis of price. In the same way, the product innovation should emphasize the difference between products and try to discourage the consumer from paying too much attention to price.

From this point of view, then, product innovation will have been most effective if the result is a product which cannot easily be compared with existing rival products. If the theory of quality choice set out earlier in this chapter turns out to be useful for explaining consumer choices, it must be that consumers can compare products as if by locating them in product space. The proliferation of characteristics implicit in the new product, however, should serve to make comparisons difficult. In this case, the quality innovation is not quite as effective at achieving the alleged objective of non-price competition as, for example, the introduction of a completely new product.

It will become apparent in later chapters—especially Chapters 5 and 6—that it is very difficult to keep the space of relevant characteristics for the analysis of quality choice and quality innovation to manageable proportions. At first this is a source of great frustration; viewed from the perspective described above, it is only to be expected.

Quality innovation: a simple exposition

As a preliminary to some formal analysis, we shall start with a simple example described by Figure 2.6. There are three qualities, produced by three different firms. Firm B, producing the middle quality, is contemplating a quality innovation. This new quality could replace the existing quality, or be an additional quality of the product; the following analysis is suitable in either case. We shall consider three possible moves for Firm B: B_1, B_2 or B_3. These correspond to: a price reduction with little change in quality; a quality improvement with little change in price; and a marked improvement in quality.

Obviously, the product B_1 is very competitive with A—see Figure 2.6 (i). Quite a wide range of consumers might prefer B_1 to A while preferring A to B. On the other hand, B_1 is less competitive with C, and relatively few consumers who prefer C to B would in turn prefer B_1 to C. Moreover, the introduction of this new quality will increase market demand if there are consumers with 'reservation' indifference curves—showing the level of utility that can be reached in buying only other goods—passing below A, B and C, but above B_1. The effect on the market can be described by the corresponding 'price function'—it can be called that even though it is not smooth and continuous. The introduction of B_1 has made the price function more convex at the low

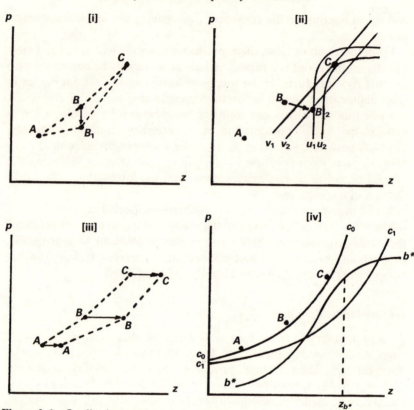

Figure 2.6 Quality innovation

quality end, but has not made much difference at the high quality end.

Contrast this with the introduction of B_2 in Figure 2.6 (ii). This is competitive with C: now a wide range of consumers may prefer B_2 to C while preferring C to B. B_2 is less competitive with A, however, and relatively few who prefer A to B would prefer B_2 to A. In this case, market demand expands when there are consumers with a demand for a good quality product at an 'average quality price'. Now, the price function becomes more convex at the high quality end.

Finally, suppose that Firm B introduces a much improved quality B_3 that is better than C. This does not compete with A or B, in the sense that any who prefer A (or B) to C will (assuming convex preferences) prefer A (or B) to B_3. Obviously, however, the new quality does compete with C. Market demand expands if there are consumers who require very high quality. This new quality has extended the domain of the price function.

The extent to which Firm *B* can improve its competitive position by these innovations depends on the distribution of indifference curves of different shapes, and the extent and nature of any rival retaliation. Broadly speaking, the less convex are the indifference curves in the neighbourhood—in other words, the nearer they are to a straight line— the greater will be improvement in *B*'s competitive position. To illustrate this, Figure 2.6 (ii) shows how the introduction of B_2 will enable *B* to capture consumers of type *v* but not of type *u*.

The effect of rival retaliation can be described by corresponding shifts of the price function. The net effect on *B*'s competitive position depends on the post-retaliation price function, as shown in Figure 2.6 (iii). As drawn, the net effect on competitive position is small; the value of the innovation depends, therefore, on the expansion of market demand.

So far, we have only shown how the firm can use quality innovation to alter the price function, and therefore demand. The optimum quality innovation naturally depends on costs. The innovation is likely to follow some reduction in costs or, more generally, an expansion in 'technological opportunity'. Following Mowery and Rosenberg (1979), we are careful not to use the tags, 'demand pull' and 'technology push' to describe innovations. The expansion of 'technological opportunity' offers scope for innovation, but the successful innovator must exploit the opportunity so as to make the demand 'pull'.

Figure 2.6 (iv) shows a downward shift in the cost function, from c_0c_0 to c_1c_1. The line b^*b^* shows a range of innovations, all of which increase the demand for *B*'s product by the same amount. Of the innovations described by b^*b^*, the optimum is the one which maximizes the distance between b^*b^* and c_1c_1. As drawn, the optimum is a markedly improved quality; this is because the most important cost reductions are for high qualities. We shall see in Chapter 3 that movements in the cost function for microelectronic components are of this sort, hence the preponderance of improved qualities in quality innovation.

Quality innovation: some formal results

The value of a quality innovation can be described simply as the extra profit it yields. For a given technology—and therefore given production costs—the value of a replacement quality innovation is:

$$\pi - \pi_0 = (px - p_0x_0) - (c(x, z) - c(x_0, z_0))$$

where p and z are the new price and quality, and x is the level of sales of the new quality; p_0, z_0, and x_0 are the initial values—which were (presumably) optimal for some earlier cost function—and $c(.,.)$ is the current cost function.

The optimum innovation is that which maximizes the extra profit, and is defined implicitly by the first order conditions:

$$x + p \frac{\partial x}{\partial p} = \frac{\partial c}{\partial x} \frac{\partial x}{\partial p}$$

$$p \frac{\partial x}{\partial z} = \frac{\partial c}{\partial x} \frac{\partial x}{\partial z} + \frac{\partial c}{\partial z} \qquad (2.18)$$

These are simply the Dorfman–Steiner (1954) conditions for optimum quality, and can be rewritten:

$$\frac{1}{e_{xp}} = \frac{p - \partial c / \partial x}{p}$$

$$\frac{e_{xz}}{e_{xp} e_{cz}} = \frac{c(x, z)}{px} \qquad (2.19)$$

where $e_{xp} = -\partial \ln x / \partial \ln p$, $e_{xz} = \partial \ln x / \partial \ln z$, and $e_{cz} = \partial \ln c / \partial \ln z$.

Following Schmalensee (1972), Lambin (1976), and others, the result can be generalized to allow for rival reaction simply by treating the elasticities e_{xp} and e_{xz} as net elasticities: that is, the elasticity of sales with respect to price and quality, net of any offsetting rival reaction provoked by changes in price and quality.

The problem with (2.19) is that we know little about the elasticities of demand with respect to price and quality, and they will depend on the density of products in quality space. In some cases it may be useful to exploit the simple insights obtained above by thinking of the quality innovation as a change in the shape of a continuous and differentiable price function. This does admittedly make the quality innovation look like a price reduction, and that was a feature of some treatments of quality that we found unsatisfactory.[17] Nevertheless, this approach provides a useful result.

For a small innovation, we can write the extra profit (neglecting some terms of second order and above) as:

$$\Delta \pi = [p(z + \delta z) + \Delta p(z)](x + \Delta x) - c(x + \Delta x, z + \Delta z)$$
$$- [p(z)x - c(x,z)]$$

Expanding by Taylor's Theorem to terms of first order, and rearranging, this becomes:

$$= [p(z) - c_x(x,z)]\Delta x + x[p'(z)\Delta z + \Delta p(z)] - c_z(x,z)\Delta z \quad (2.20)$$

The second and third terms simply represent the increment to revenue and costs (and therefore to profit) at a given level of sales; these can be calculated fairly easily. The first term represents the increment to profit from extra sales; this is harder to calculate, depending as it does on changes in the shape of the price function, and the density of consumers with different types of preferences. Nevertheless, we can obtain a relatively simple expression for Δx, the change in sales.

We derived in equation (2.6) above an expression for aggregate demand for different qualities. We modify it slightly here to write the aggregate demand for quality z^* as:

$$F(z^*) = \int_\theta x(\theta)\, \varepsilon_{z(\theta)} f(\theta)\, \varepsilon_{z^*} d\theta \quad (2.21)$$

where θ is used to index the consumers, $z(\theta)$ and $x(\theta)$ are the quality and quantity choices of consumers of type θ, $f(\theta)$ is a density function, and $\varepsilon_{z(\theta)}$ and ε_{z^*} are point measures of unit mass at $z(\theta)$ and z^* respectively. The point measures serve to sort out all the consumers for whom $z(\theta) = z^*$, and then their individual demands are aggregated to obtain $F(z^*)$.

The effect of any change in $p(.)$ on demand for a particular quality is easily obtained. For a fixed density function,[18] the increment to $F(z^*)$ is given by:

$$\delta F(z^*) = \int_\theta \delta_{x(\theta)}\, \varepsilon_{z(\theta)} f(\theta)\, \varepsilon_{z^*}\, d\theta + \int_\theta x(\theta)\, \frac{\delta\varepsilon_{z(\theta)}}{\delta z(\theta)}\, \delta z(\theta) f(\theta)\, \varepsilon_{z^*}\, d\theta \quad (2.22)$$

The second term involves a term $[\delta\varepsilon_{z(\theta)}/\delta z(\theta)]\delta z(\theta)$. This is simply $\varepsilon_{z(\theta)+\delta z(\theta)} - \varepsilon_{z(\theta)}$, and shows how individual consumers switch from one quality to another.

This result is particularly pleasing, as it separates the increment to aggregate demand for a particular quality into two parts. The first term in a sense represents the expansion of market demand, while the second term may be taken to represent the improvement of competitive position. Thus the first term is the sum of increments to individuals' demands at the particular quality, while the second term captures all the individuals who shift from one quality to another. We have already seen how these individual choices depend on changes in the price function (see equation (2.5) above).

If a firm makes a quality innovation, and rivals do not retaliate, then the result is to reduce the slope of the price function immediately below the quality innovation, and to increase the slope immediately above the quality innovation. Those consumers who were buying a quality just below this new quality innovation will find that the marginal price of quality has fallen, and the substitution effect will lead them to buy a higher quality. On the other hand, those consumers who were buying a quality just above the new quality innovation will find that the marginal price of quality has risen, and the substitution effect will lead them to buy a lower quality. Thus the quality innovation has the effect of 'drawing in' consumers from both sides; this is the improvement in competitive position.

If, however, the firm's rivals do retaliate to neutralize the original innovation by corresponding quality innovations, then these local changes in the slope of the price function will be smoothed out. The net result may be that the post-retaliation price function is of the same shape as the original price function, but just a little lower.

2.6 The theory of spatial and product competition

We have seen that the value of a quality innovation depends on whether rival firms make corresponding innovations. The optimum quality innovation must depend, therefore, on the nature of competition in product space. For that reason, we present here a brief review of some of the main themes in the literature on spatial and product competition theory, outlining their predictions for the nature of spatial and product competition, and stressing the key assumptions on which these predictions depend. This section is based on Swann (1985a), and makes no pretence at comprehensiveness; very useful (though by their own admission 'selective') surveys are provided by Graitson (1982) and Keyfitz (1981), *inter alia*.

Much of what follows refers to location in geographical space but, as we have seen above, quality choice can be seen as location in product or characteristics space. It is not surprising, therefore, that many economists have thought that models suitable for analysis of geographical location may also be suitable for the analysis of product 'location'.

There can be problems, however, in assuming that results which apply to geographical space will automatically apply to product space; the essential point is that in geographical space there is usually a natural (Euclidean) metric, while in product space, there need not be.

Hotelling's analysis of pure spatial competition

The celebrated analysis by Hotelling (1929) refers to a simple duopoly model of pure spatial competition along a linear market. In this model, consumers have inelastic demand but buy from the nearest seller: they are assumed to have no doubt about which is the nearest seller. Sellers are able to relocate freely, and they assume that their rival will not react to any such relocation. Hotelling demonstrated that the model would have a single equilibrium where the two sellers were back-to-back in the middle of their market. Some writers conjectured that clustering of this sort might prove to be a pervasive equilibrium property of more general spatial models, but subsequent work suggests that the famous result is sensitive to the particular assumptions made.

Extensions to Hotelling's original analysis have been made in several directions. Here we consider the effects of the following features: (a) a greater number of competing firms; (b) location on a plane rather than a line; (c) relaxing the assumption of inelastic demand; (d) introducing seller relocation costs; (e) consumer inability to distinguish between very similar goods; (f) non-zero conjectural variations; and finally (g) 'agglomeration' economies, or mutual economies accruing to sellers who locate close to each other.

(a) More Firms

Lerner and Singer (1937), Eaton and Lipsey (1975), Shaked (1975), and Graitson (1982), *inter alia*, have looked at the question of increasing the number of competing firms. Lerner and Singer showed that when a third firm entered the same linear market, it would locate itself next to the two existing firms so as to sandwich one of them in the middle. This, however, would not be a stable position as the sandwiched firm would be starved of its market share, and would leapfrog into the largest open segment of the market. This process of leapfrogging would continue indefinitely: there is no Nash equilibrium with three firms in a linear market.

With four firms, the equilibrium will have the firms gathered in two back-to-back pairs at the quartiles. For five firms, the equilibrium will have one singleton located at the middle of the market, and two back-to-back pairs located at the first and fifth sextiles, in such a way as to equalize market shares. For more firms, the equilibrium is not unique, but involves some pairing.

(b) Location in a plane
The extension of Hotelling's analysis to location in two-dimensional space has proved to be rather difficult. Here, any equilibrium must be robust not only to movements up and down a line, but also to diagonal movements. Indeed, Eaton and Lipsey (1975) and Shaked (1975) found that in many cases equilibrium does not exist or is not unique. Nevertheless, Eaton and Lipsey did find that there was a tendency for clusters to emerge; this occurs especially when firms have open spaces on one side of them, so that there is no loss from moving towards the cluster.

(c) Elastic demand
Lerner and Singer (1937) relaxed Hotelling's assumption of inelastic demand, by introducing a reservation price. The outcome now depends on the length of the line and transport costs. The maximum length of each seller's market depends on the size of transport costs in relation to the reservation price. If the line is long enough, both sellers can act as independent monopolists, but if not central clustering will occur.

(d) Relocation costs and entry deterrence
Hay (1976) and Rothschild (1976) extended the analysis to the case where relocation is costly, and firms take a long-term view of location. At the planning stage, firms must take into account the probable location decisions of subsequent entrants. Faced with a decision of where to locate on a line between two other firms, the entrant recognizes that if it locates beside an existing firm it will leave an attractive wide-open space for a subsequent entrant. This model leads to a dispersion of firms. The form of this dispersion depends on the distribution of demand: the density of firms will be greatest where demand is densest. Moreover, in a growing market the spacing will not necessarily be regular.

There are two important issues here: the introduction of relocation costs, and the long-term or entry-deterring view of location. Other things being equal, the existence of relocation costs will encourage the firm to locate so as to minimize the risk of enforced relocation. In Hay's paper, competitive entry could force an established firm to relocate, so the firm locates to deter entry, but as we see below this is not the only context in which relocation costs may be important.

The strategy of locating to deter entry provides an explanation (if not the only possible explanation) of proliferation, or simultaneous location in several places. This is of considerable importance in product competition—see Shaw (1982 a and b), Scherer (1979) and Schmalensee (1978).

(e) Consumer confusion

Devletoglou (1965) examined the question of consumer inability to distinguish between similar products. If a consumer finds himself almost equidistant from the two nearest sellers, his custom might in practice alternate between them in a random way. If the two sellers are located back to back, then all consumers will find there is little to choose between the sellers. If, on the other hand, the two sellers are located well apart, only a relatively small number of consumers will find the two sellers equally satisfactory. Devletoglou argued, therefore, that a desire to minimize sales uncertainty would encourage sellers to locate apart. This will be especially relevant if there are high relocation costs.

(f) Non-zero conjectural variations

Smithies (1941) and, more recently, Gannon (1973), Eaton (1972), and others have examined the matter of non-zero conjectural variations. Smithies suggested that the prospect of rival reaction would prevent a seller from moving towards a cluster, but Eaton found that the outcome depends on the length of the market. If the market is short enough, the clustering can survive, but in a wide-open market firms locate apart. Gannon found that the outcome with non-zero conjectural variations depends on the elasticity of demand: for given conjectures, clustering can still survive so long as demand is sufficiently inelastic. Nevertheless, when relocation costs are high, firms may be sufficiently keen to avoid the risk of enforced relocation that they locate to minimize the risk of rival reaction.

As Keyfitz (1981) points out, these results—and those mentioned in (c) above—illustrate an essential feature of the Hotelling model. In Hotelling's analysis, the sellers do not perceive any cost in moving toward the cluster.

(g) Agglomeration economies

The final extension is the introduction of agglomeration economies—or mutual economies of adjacent location. Various writers have made reference to them—for example, Weber (1929), Nelson (1958), Stahl and Varaiya (1978), Webber (1972)—but as Graitson (1982) has suggested, there is room for further integration of such agglomeration economies into the models of location discussed above.

In the context of geographical location, these agglomeration economies are of three sorts:

(1) the shared infrastructure available to firms locating close to each other—transport, communications, and ease of supply;
(2) the informational externality about the density of demand or the technical feasibility of production which accrues to the prospective entrant who sees an established firm trading profitably at a particular location—see Stahl and Varaiya (1978);
(3) the reduction of consumer search costs, beneficial for total market demand—a striking example of this is to be found in the clustering of antique shops.

How do such agglomeration economies operate for location in product space? Particular examples that are found in microprocessors will be discussed in Chapter 6; in general it is fairly easy to find examples similar to (1) and (2) above, but examples comparable to (3) are harder to envisage. Concerning (1), 'infrastructure', these are really standardization economies. A trivial example is that the firm making non-standard sizes of paper may find that the product does not sell because it does not fit into standard envelopes, ring-binders, or photocopiers. With regard to (2), informational externality, one firm's success in producing and selling a particular design demonstrates to the potential entrant the feasibility of production and the strength of demand.

These agglomeration economies are clearly an incentive for clustering. The existence of informational externalities implies that from one point of view location in a cluster is less risky—contrast this with the arguments above. The existence of high relocation costs would again encourage the firm to locate so as to minimize the risk of enforced relocation, but from this point of view that risk is reduced by locating in a cluster.[19] We cannot say a priori whether agglomeration economies would prove a more important force than the opposing forces against clustering. Nevertheless, we might conjecture that, especially for location in product space, firms locate sufficiently closely (in some dimensions) to benefit from these economies, but differentiate the product in other ways (other dimensions).

Summary

Four main points emerge from this very brief review. Firstly, extending the Hotelling analysis to more sellers and higher dimension spaces introduces difficulties with the uniqueness and sometimes the existence of equilibrium. Nevertheless, the tendency to cluster does not necessarily disappear. Secondly, Hotelling's clustering result does seem to be sensitive to some of the assumptions he makes. In particular, the tendency to cluster can break down when allowance is made for elastic demand, relocation costs, sales uncertainty arising from the consumer's inability to distinguish between close sellers, and non-zero conjectural variations. Thirdly, the existence of agglomeration economies can provide an additional incentive to cluster, not present in Hotelling's analysis. Finally, relocation costs are seen to play a central role in the analysis. If relocation costs are high, firms will locate so as to reduce the risk of enforced relocation. If, for example, rival reaction is seen as the greatest risk, firms locate apart, but if doubts about market demand or technical feasibility are paramount, then firms will cluster.

Notes

1. Power (1941). The handbook referred to is Pegolotti's *Pratica della Mercatura* (early fourteenth century).
2. *Principles of Economics*, Book III, Chapter ii, Section 1. See also Chapter iv, Sections 4 and 7.
3. In later work, Gorman (1976) and Lancaster (1979) discuss the problems caused by additivity.
4. Ironically, power consumption is additive if defined as a 'bad', but not if defined as a good. The same is true of size.
5. The theorem states—among other things—that the intersection of two overlapping separable sets is also separable.
6. Houthakker (1952) also made some explorations along these lines.
7. There is an additional difficulty: if there is price discrimination, so that a particular quality is sold at various different prices, then a point in the domain (quality space) could map to various points in the range (prices). This problem disappears if we use a minimum price function: if the same variety is available at a number of prices, the function takes the value of the minimum price. In the same way, non-monotonicities can be eliminated by removing the dominated varieties—that is, the varieties that can be bettered at no higher cost. This is the method used in Chapter 5.

8. We assume that this inversion is possible.
9. Rosen (1974) suggests a similar differential demand equation.
10. Davies (1979) and Stoneman (1983) give very detailed discussions of the various themes in the analysis of diffusion.
11. In this way, the existence of pure diffusion can serve to identify demand curves (Swann, 1985d).
12. Aitchison and Brown (1957) have given many examples of the use of quasi Engel curves. See also Cramer (1958).
13. This is rather different from the neoclassical demand for durables; see Diewert (1974), in which the existence of good second-hand markets makes the purchase of a durable good little different from the purchase of a non-durable.
14. To allow for resale, it would be necessary to introduce second-hand price functions.
15. The whole argument can be generalized to reservation qualities, and reservation price/quality combinations.
16. The second order condition is:

$$[(h + r)^2 v(t) - (q + r)^2 p(t)]e^{-rt} < 0.$$

Combining this with the first order condition, we obtain:

$$[(h + r) - (q + r)](q + r)p(t)e^{-rt} < 0$$

which requires $q > h$.
17. A discrete approach is offered by the marketing models of brand share; see for example Hauser and Gaskin (1984), Kakamura and Srivastava (1984), and Gavish *et al.* (1983). An alternative approach is the discrete measurement of product competitiveness; see Swann (1985b).
18. We could allow for changes in the density function—pure diffusion in effect—by introducing a third term in the total differential.
19. As Webber (1972) puts it, '. . . the location decisions of uncertain firms are more conservative than those made by certain firms'.

3 Microelectronic Technology: The Measurement of Quality and The Economics of Design

This chapter can be seen as an attempt to look behind the products, indifference curves and cost curves of the last chapter. Thus, we describe microelectronic technology and the uses to which it can be put, we present a framework which can be used to describe the value of quality improvements to the user, and we describe the costs of production and how they depend on product quality. The technology is taken to be the set of basic components: the producers are those who produce basic components, while consumers are all those (system manufacturers, original equipment manufacturers,[1] and end users) who make some use of these basic components.

Section 3.1 describes the technology and its uses. In a sense, many applications of digital microelectronics can be seen as computer systems, even if the computer is a small part of the system. For this reason, the techniques of computer system measurement—developed by computer scientists to analyze the performance of large computer systems— can be useful for describing the value of improvements in the technology for any particular application. A few of the tools are described in Section 3.2.

To use the analysis of Chapter 2, we must isolate a few important characteristics of microelectronic technology. In fact, rather a lot of parameters are required to describe the technology, but they are inter-related. By considering some elementary physics, we shall see in Section 3.3 that advances in miniaturization lead at the same time to reductions in power consumption and cost, and to increases in speed and capacity.

The rest of the chapter is concerned with the economics of manufacture and design. Section 3.4 gives a concise description of the production process for microelectronic components. Section 3.5 presents a simple model of production costs, which can be used to derive optimum 'chip' sizes. Finally, Section 3.6 describes some of the economics of design, concentrating on the relationship between the functions performed by a component and the 'chip' size.

3.1 The technology and its uses

By microelectronic components, we mean devices that contain a large number of transistors and diodes integrated into one device. The components are of very small dimensions, and a very high packing density is achieved by eliminating individual containers and connecting wires. More specifically, we shall be talking about semiconductor components; that is, devices made of semiconductor materials, in particular, silicon.

There are two types of device: the analog, where signals are of the continuously variable type that we have in speech, music, etc., and the digital, where signals are coded (almost invariably) in binary form. In analog devices, the output of a transistor is continuously variable; ideally, the output function is linear in the input. In digital devices, the transistor acts simply as a conditional switch; it is either on or off, depending on the input. Analog devices tend to require very few transistors to carry out their function,[2] but the transistors must be of high quality. Digital devices, on the other hand, require rather more transistors, but they can be of lower quality.

In this study, our main interest is in digital devices. The simplest digital integrated circuits—produced from the early 1960s onwards—are gates; these are purely logical devices. In Boolean algebra there are *and, or, nand, nor* functions; so it is with gates. These are the logical building blocks,[3] which are combined to construct any complex logical function. With analog devices, design is largely connected with electrical matters; with digital devices, on the other hand, logical matters are the primary concern.

Some simple electronic systems, especially early control systems, are 'hard-wired'; that is to say, their function was fixed into the circuit and could not be changed short of dismantling and reassembly. At that time, components were expensive and in order to economize on components it was best to define the required features of any circuit as precisely as possible, and then to choose the minimum number of components to fulfil that role.

The situation has changed, especially in the 1970s. With integrated electronics, components have become relatively cheap, and it has become possible to make generous use of components in order to achieve standardization in parts and flexibility in design.[4] Often, therefore, it is cheaper to design a system that operates by stored program control; that is, its function can be modified by changing the control program. In this sense, many applications of microelectronics can be viewed as small computer systems.

The Von Neumann design still forms the basis of operation for most computer systems from the largest mainframes to the smallest stored program control system.[5] In this design, the central processor follows instructions from program memory, takes data from data memory, calculates logical or arithmetic functions from these data, and stores the new results back in data memory.

System requirements

The number of gates and the amount of memory required are naturally dependent on the complexity of the system, the number of inputs, the number of outputs, the complexity of logical and arithmetic functions to be computed, and the number of these functions. Besides the capacity requirements there will be other requirements, involving the speed at which operations must be done, how reliable the system must be, and how much power consumption can be allowed.

It is usual, for example, to distinguish between real-time and non real-time systems. Real-time systems have to function to a fairly strict external timetable. While it may not be busy all the time, the real-time system must be able to complete a particular workload in a particular time. Time is 'real' because it is externally measured, and not purely internal. Non real-time systems, on the other hand, are allowed to accumulate a backlog of long (though not infinite) length. Work can be shifted from peak times to slack times; in effect, then, there is no peak time. Electricity supply is a good example of a real-time system, while purely batch computing is a good example of a not very real-time system. The distinction will be made clearer when a few concepts in computer system measurement have been explained in Section 3.2.

Naturally an electronic control system requires not only logical components, but also a logical design. For stored program control systems, this is the program or applications software. The software complexity depends on the number and sequence of operations to be done, and the complexity of these operations. So does the cost of producing the software, though it seems unlikely that the cost of software production is proportional to, or even linear in, software complexity.

Table 3.1   Applications of microelectronics

Data processing and office automation
      Computer systems
      CAD/CAM equipment
      Data storage systems
      Data terminals
      Input/Output peripherals
      Copying equipment
      Word-processing systems
      Source data collection

Consumer equipment
      Consumer audio equipment
      Consumer video equipment
      Automative electronics

Test and measurement equipment
      Automated test equipment
      General test instrumentation
      Analytical instruments
      Medical equipment

Communication equipment
      Data communications
      Facsimile terminals
      Pocket pagers
      Radar equipment
      Radio & TV equipment
      Telecommunications

Industrial equipment
      Energy-management systems
      Inspection systems
      Motor and other controls
      Numerical control systems
      Process control equipment
      Robot systems
      Lasers and ultrasonics

Government electronics
      Defence communications
      Electronics in aircraft
      Electronics in missiles

Electronic components put together as a system are quite useless unless a system of input and output is devised. For the computer, inputs are card readers, terminals, tapes, disks, etc., while outputs are usually line printers, terminals, tapes, cards, disks, etc. For control applications, input and output devices are more varied. In watches, the inputs are a few buttons and a crystal; in the calculator, the inputs are keys; in engine control, the inputs are various sensors, transducers, while the outputs are activators and display components. Barron and Curnow (1979, p. 77) describe the importance of input and output thus:

As the scale of the computer is reduced . . . the importance of the internal operation declines in comparison with the importance of the interface operation. It is as though the computer could be represented by a circle, with the interior for internal processing, and the circumference as the interface. As the size of the circle is reduced, so the properties of the boundary come to dominate.

Indeed, $2\pi r/\pi r^2 = 2/r$. According to this simple analogy, the relative importance of interface is inversely proportional to the square root of a computer's system size.

For some applications—see the example of car engine control in Chapter 8—the interface is very important indeed. By that we do not mean the electronic interface components, but rather the transducers, activators, power transistors, etc. In many cases it is technical difficulties with these interface components, rather than the electronics itself, that hampers the development of microelectronic control systems for a particular application.

Applications

Like money, what the technology is may best be described by what it does. A huge number of applications have already been found, and many more wait to be found. Table 3.1 shows some of the most important applications of microelectronic components.

3.2 Computer system measurement

Some analytical tools have proved useful for the process of measurement. We mention some of them here; for a fuller discussion, reference is made to Beizer (1978). The performance of a given computer system is described by *throughput, delay,* and *resources,* or analogously by *subjective* and *objective* work rates, and by *processing* rates.

The resources are the various functional components of the system; the delay is the time that the system takes to perform certain operations; the throughput is the total work done by the system in unit time. The subjective rate is the work rate perceived by the user submitting a single item of work; from obvious considerations, it is equal to the inverse of delay. The objective work rate is simply the throughput, while the processing rate is the maximum work rate that can be achieved with given resources.

System design is, in a sense, the art of assembling various resources to do certain sorts of work, with the performance of the system of given resources measured by so-called throughput-delay curves, or subjective rate/objective rate curves. The throughput-delay curves show, for a particular system with particular resources, the system delay experienced at different levels of throughput. Likewise, the subjective rate/ objective rate curve shows for a particular system with a particular processing rate the subjective work rate experienced at different objective rates.

The relationship between throughput and delay depends on the nature of the system. For some very simple systems where work arrives at a constant (non-stochastic) rate along one channel, delay may be constant below the maximum throughput, but at that maximum throughput it becomes infinite. That is, an ever-increasing backlog of work will form. For some more complex systems, delay may be a decreasing function of unconsumed resources, becoming infinite when resources are saturated. A rather useful class of throughput-delay curves is described by:

$$\text{Delay} = (T_{\text{max}} - T)^{-1/k}$$

where T_{max} is the maximum throughput, T is the actual throughput, and k is some constant parameter. For $k \to \infty$, this is the simple case of constant delay up to the maximum throughput. For $k = 1$, a case of particular interest to Beizer (1978), delay is inversely proportional to unconsumed resources, or alternatively:

$$\text{subjective rate} = \text{processing rate} - \text{objective rate}$$

The benefits of quality innovation to a computer system can be measured in terms of shifts in the throughput-delay curves (as well as the reductions in power consumption and size). For different systems, the shifts would be rather different—this gives rise to a conventional

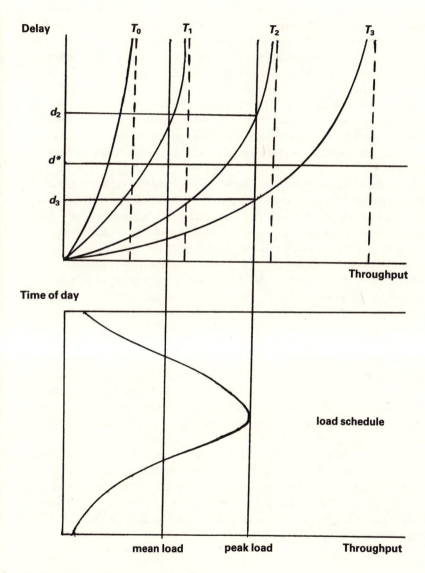

Figure 3.1 Throughput-delay curves

index number problem. The total benefit of quality innovation, moreover, would have to take account of any new systems that are used.

For some sorts of system, the throughput-delay curve may be improved simply by the use of extra resources. An example of this is the use of co-processors to share the processing load. In such a case the combination of existing products gives the same result as improvements in product quality. This is not always true, however, for if two processors would have to share common resources which they use a lot, then the system may be constrained by these resources, and the addition of an extra processor may make no difference. Furthermore, for obvious reasons, quality innovations such as miniaturization and reductions in power consumption, cannot be simulated by the combination of existing resources.

With these throughput-delay curves, it is easy to see the distinction between real time and non real-time. In Figure 3.1, four throughput-delay curves are given which represent the performance obtained from four versions of a system using different resources or technology of different qualities. The curves are the throughput-delay curves, and the dotted lines are their asymptotes, at the maximum throughput. In the lower half of the diagram, a load schedule for the computer system is presented; the peak load and 'daily' mean load are shown.

System T_0 cannot even meet the mean load; it will suffer an ever-increasing backlog. System T_1 can meet the mean load, but cannot meet the peak load; it will cope so long as work can be rescheduled. But rescheduling is not possible in a real-time system, only in a non real-time system. System T_2 can meet the peak load: it can therefore provide a real-time system. It may be, however, that the maximum acceptable delay is given by d^*; T_2 will experience a delay of d_2 ($>d^*$) at peak load. Only T_3 can provide a real-time system with worst-case delay (d_3) below the maximum acceptable (d^*).

We have seen that electronic components can make small computer systems, and that these are inherently very flexible. The logical operations of any mechanical control system could be carried out by a computer system, and indeed the computer would be able to add many features as it can take account of many more inputs and control many more outputs.

3.3 Some fundamental relationships between technology parameters

This is not the place to describe the physics of semiconductor devices (see Hoenissen and Mead, 1972; Folberth and Bleher, 1979), but it is very important to understand why there are certain intrinsic relationships between some of the technology parameters.

There are two sorts of transistor in integrated electronics, bipolar and metal oxide silicon (MOS). The bipolar takes a current input to open (so to speak) a low resistance ($<100\Omega$) path between emitter and collector. The MOS takes a voltage input to open a rather higher resistance path ($1-10$ KΩ). The speeds at which the two types of transistor work are related to their ability to discharge output node capacitances quickly. Given that they have similar node capacitances, that depends on the switch transconductance, a function of—amongst other things—the path resistance. Bipolar transistors typically have some twenty times higher transconductance than MOS (Wise *et al.*, 1980, Section 2.2.4). Moreover, voltage swings have to be several times larger for MOS, and that increases the speed differential.

The node capacitances are proportional to the sizes of elementary devices, and the interconnecting line lengths. Large capacitances imply not only slow speeds, but also higher power dissipation. Indeed, these capacitances determine the power-delay product, a frequently quoted parameter. For any logical operation, a capacitor must be discharged; the faster it is done, the higher the power dissipation. The power-delay product is, in effect, the sum of node capacitances in a gate.

Miniaturization, then, leads directly to greater speeds (because of shorter paths), lower node capacitances (lower power-delay product), and higher component density (lower component cost). Moreover, it

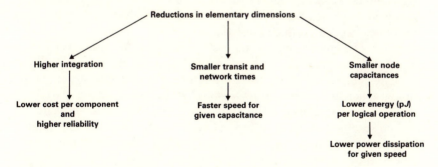

Figure 3.2   Fundamental relationships between technology parameters

makes for more reliable components (at least up to a certain degree of miniaturization). On the other hand, high density requires lower voltages, but there are lower bounds to these. Besides, power considerations can put limitations on attainable density, and network synchronization considerations can constrain the speed benefits of higher density.

These interrelationships between technology parameters are summarized in Figure 3.2. They arise because of fundamental aspects of semiconductor physics; several others follow because of engineering constraints, as we shall see below.

3.4 The manufacture of integrated circuits

To help understand the economics of manufacture and design, it is useful to have a brief review of the process used to produce integrated circuits—for further details, reference is made to Oldham (1977), Wise *et al.* (1980), Wilson *et al.* (1980), Ide (1982), and on a rather technical level, Mead and Conway (1980).

The essence of the techniques used for making integrated circuits have not changed since the early days of integrated circuits. The main technique is the planar process combined with photolithography. The planar process builds circuits by growing a stack of cross-section layers of silicon dioxide on a slice of pure silicon. From the early days, photolithography has been used to imprint the right patterns on to these layers, though new alternatives are appearing.

For each layer the process is much the same, and the cycle is repeated several times; we describe the first cycle. A pure slice of silicon is heated in a furnace in the presence of oxygen and is oxidized. Oxides of silicon are excellent insulators, and a good layer of oxide will serve to insulate adjacent cross-section layers unless a section of the oxide layer is removed. The idea is to cut out part of the insulating oxide layer, and introduce impurities which cause the exposed silicon to act as a semiconductor.[6] This cutting out is achieved by covering the oxide layer with a liquid called photoresist; this has the property that those parts exposed to light—corresponding to the transparent parts sections of the photolithographic mask (see below)—will harden, while those parts not exposed can be etched away. Impurities are introduced through the etched sections, either by diffusion (heating in the presence of a vapour of the impurity) or by ion implantation (literally firing ions at the surface so that they dig in).

The cycle is repeated a number of times, the precise number depending on the nature of the circuit and the technology (in engineer's parlance, e.g. MOS, bipolar) used. Sometimes the oxidization and etching are done alone and the diffusion or implantation step is left out. The last step involves melting a layer of aluminium over the surface, and etching out the connecting paths.

In the actual production process a mask contains not just one circuit, but a large number. At present, a single circuit will not be more than about 5–10mm square, for reasons that will become clear later. On a 100mm-diameter slice, neglecting edge dropout, that means some 100–300 separate circuits per slice. These will all be quite self-contained, and they are tested individually. A large number fail this test—80 to 90 per cent or more—for reasons that will again become clear later.

This preliminary test is usually not exhaustive, and those chips that pass the first test are (after being individually packaged) subjected to a second and more thorough test. For a circuit as complex as a microprocessor, however, this second test is by no means exhaustive either; indeed, it is arguable that a completely exhaustive test is nearly impossible.

3.5 The economics of manufacture

From the discussion in the previous section, it is evident that processing costs per wafer depend on the number of masking and diffusion steps. More precisely, processing cost per wafer is given by:

$$c_1 m + c_2 d + T \tag{3.1}$$

where m is the number of masking steps, d is the number of diffusion or implantation steps, T is the cost of a bulk test per wafer, and c_1 and c_2 are the marginal costs per masking and diffusion step respectively. Packaging and final test costs per chip depend on the complexity of the chip and the number of contacts per chip. The average cost of a working chip must, therefore, depend on the proportion that fail the two tests. It is the first test that counts here; the final test does not usually reject many more, and for simplicity we shall assume that the yield of this final test is unity.

There are at least three reasons why a chip may be a 'dud', even though the chip and mask design are workable. The first is that some areas of the silicon slice have impurities, but this possibility is not very important in practice. The second is that the masks have not been aligned properly, which would tend to ruin an entire wafer. Typically, however, engineers define the technology parameters so that this does not happen; at any 'state of the art', a certain alignment tolerance is either feasible or not feasible. Thirdly, and by far the most important in practice, random photographic defects in the masks—such as dust particles—introduce defects in the chip.

Suppose that in some very small unit area of a mask there will either be one defect with (very small) probability f, or no defects with probability $1-f$. Suppose, too, that the occurrence of defects in adjacent unit areas are independent events. Finally, assume that to obtain a working chip, each mask must be free of defects in the area corresponding to that chip. Then we can derive the yield function as follows.[7] If the chip area in the very small units is A, then the probability of no defects in that area of the mask corresponding to the chip is $(1-f)$. For n masks, the probability of no defects and therefore the probability of a working chip is $(1-f)^{nA}$. For very small f, which we have here, this can be approximated by e^{-nfA}.[8] The yield of working chips will then fall exponentially with the expected number of defects per chip multiplied by the number of masks n. Likewise, the cost of a working chip rises exponentially since cost per working chip equals cost per chip divided by the yield of working chips.

From all this it is clear that the cost for a working chip of area A is:

$$\frac{[c_1 m + c_2 d + T]}{S} \cdot A e^{nfA} \tag{3.2}$$

where S is the slice area. To this we add packaging costs, a function of chip area $P(A)$.

Given this cost function, it is possible to calculate optimum chip sizes.[9] Naturally, the optimum will depend on the value attached to area, and that depends on required functional capacity, which is still to be discussed. One special case which is useful as a benchmark, and often as a lower limit for optimum chip size, is the case where the user has some fixed requirement for functional complexity, and wishes to minimize the cost of his system, but is indifferent to the number of packages over which his silicon is spread. This implies that he is indifferent to size, reliability, cost of assembly, and quite possibly speed; it is therefore a somewhat unrealistic assumption, but a benchmark all the same. Then the optimum chip size is the one which minimizes the cost of unit

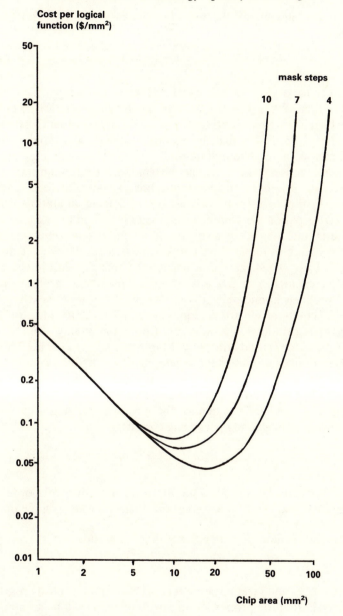

Figure 3.3 Unit cost per logical function

functional complexity, or the average cost of unit area. That is, it minimizes:

$$\frac{1}{A} \cdot \frac{[c_1 m + c_2 d + T]}{S} \cdot A e^{nfA} + \frac{P(A)}{A} \qquad (3.3)$$

with respect to A. Figure 3.3 shows the average cost per unit as a function of area. What is particularly striking for the numerical example given—which is based on representative values of the parameters given in Wise *et al.* (1980)[10]—is that the average cost rises very rapidly when area is increased above the optimum.

The yield function sets a fairly narrow band on the optimum chip size, but there can be other considerations. For example, there is a total power dissipation constraint because of packaging limitations. The maximum dissipation per chip in air is generally agreed to be about one or two watts; this may act as a constraint on chip size in some cases.

We can use this simple model to obtain two results alluded to in Chapter 2. First, we suggested in Section 2.5 that the shift in the cost curve depicted in Figure 2.6 was typical of the shifts resulting from technical progress in microelectronics. We shall see in the next section that the functions of electronic components all take up space on the chip, and thus chip area is a measure of potential quality—and actual quality if the space is used efficiently. Moreover, we shall see in Chapter 4 that one of the most important developments in the technology since the 1960s has been an increase in density: that is, an increase in the number of gates that can be put in a unit area of silicon.

Writing $z = gA$, where z is quality and g is gates per unit area, (3.2) can be rewritten (neglecting packaging costs):

$$c = c_0 \frac{z}{g} e^{nfz/g} \qquad (3.4)$$

where c_0 is simply $(c_1 m + c_2 d + T)/S$. If we assume to a first order of approximation that c_0 and n are constant, then it is easy to show that:

$$\frac{d\ln c}{dt} = -\frac{d\ln g}{dt} + \frac{znf}{g}\frac{d\ln f}{dt} - \frac{znf}{g}\frac{d\ln g}{dt} \qquad (3.5)$$

Since g increases and f (faults per unit area) falls with technical progress, then it is clear that the proportionate cost reductions will be greater for high-quality components (with many gates). This is the justification for Figure 2.6 (iv).

A second result, equation (2.14), was mentioned in Section 2.4 when discussing the timing of purchases: we had to evaluate $(r - \mathrm{d}\ln p/\mathrm{d}t)/(\mathrm{d}\ln p/\mathrm{d}z)$, where r was a discount rate. To do this we require (3.5), and an expression for $\mathrm{d}\ln c/\mathrm{d}\ln z$. From (3.2), again neglecting packaging costs, we obtain:

$$\frac{\mathrm{d}\ln c}{\mathrm{d}z} = \frac{1}{z}\left[1 + \frac{nfz}{g}\right] \tag{3.6}$$

With two further assumptions, we can obtain (2.14). First, we assume that manufacturers apply a fixed percentage mark-up; then $\mathrm{d}\ln p/\mathrm{d}t = \mathrm{d}\ln c/\mathrm{d}t$. Second, we assume that the yield of working chips is about 13 per cent. Since $z=gA$, and yield $= \mathrm{e}^{-nfA}$, then $nfz/g \approx 2$. In that case, we combine (3.5) and (3.6) to obtain:

$$\frac{r - \mathrm{d}\ln p/\mathrm{d}t}{\mathrm{d}\ln p/\mathrm{d}z} = z\left[\frac{\mathrm{d}\ln g}{\mathrm{d}t} - \frac{2}{3}\frac{\mathrm{d}\ln f}{\mathrm{d}t} + \frac{r}{3}\right] \tag{3.7}$$

Equation (2.14) follows in an obvious manner.

3.6 From functional design to chip design

So much for the production process and the choice of chip size. We now turn to the questions of functional design, mask layout design, and choice of technology. The principal points that have to be discussed are contained in Figure 3.4. We have already dealt with the relationship between chip area and integrated circuit cost, and how that relationship depends on the complexity of the photolithographic process. That is depicted in the bottom right-hand corner of the diagram. In this section we deal with the rest of the diagram.

In the bottom half of the diagram the various boxes describe the various features of the integrated circuit. Double lines imply a functional relationship between the contents of two boxes; single lines imply the effect of some technology parameter on a functional relationship. In the top half of the diagram are the technology parameters, where we mean by technology what the electronic engineer refers to—for example, pMOS, nMOS, TTL, ECL, etc. It is argued that all these technologies can be dealt with in a common framework, where different technologies have different values for these parameters.

We start with the relationship between functional design and chip area. The functional design is in terms of building blocks such as

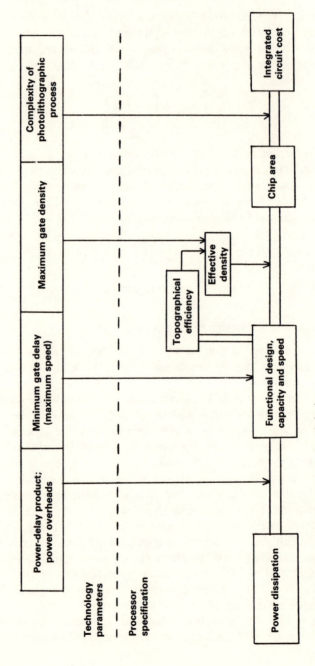

Figure 3.4   The economics of functional design

instruction decoders, registers, arithmetic and logic units, memory, and so on. This has to be converted into a logical design, in terms of gates and memory cells, and then to a circuit design in terms of transistors. The layout or topography of the circuit must be arranged so that it is suitable to transfer on to a chip using the planar process and photo-lithography. The layout is translated into a set of masks for the photo-lithography.

For a particular functional design and capacity, the required chip area will depend on two things: first, the space required for the necessary components, which depends on the maximum gate density for the technology chosen; and second, the space required for connecting leads. A topographically efficient layout will minimize the proportion of chip area that is taken up by connecting leads. The efficiency that can be achieved depends on the nature of the circuit; random logic, as found in some parts of a microprocessor, can have a topography five times less efficient—that is, five times less dense—than regular logic such as that used in a memory array (Barron and Curnow, 1979, p. 70).

Regularity is very important in design. Functions that can be laid out in a regular way make efficient use of the chip area. When high levels of integration are desirable, chip area is at a premium; it is sometimes referred to as 'real estate'. To say, then, that a certain function requires so many transistors is misleading;[11] more important is the space they take up. Barron (1978) suggests that a small processor may require a similar area to 4–8 kilobits of memory; larger processors require the space of 16 kilobits. Interfacing circuitry is particularly inefficient; 16 bits of interface require equivalent space to one small processor.

Different technologies (in the engineer's sense) offer different maximum densities not because of differences in fundamental resolutions but because of differences in sizes of elementary components.[12]

Attention to topographical efficiency is a relatively recent concern. In the early days of computer design, the switch was the costly component, while wires were cheap (Sutherland and Mead, 1977). Efficient design—as embodied in the now practically obsolete switching theory—mini-mized the number of switches, but paid little attention to economy in connecting wires (topographical efficiency). Today, the switch takes minimal chip space, while connectors take a lot of space.

The methods used to ensure efficiency in topography have been rather *ad hoc*, but *'ad hoc'* should not be interpreted in a pejor-ative sense: some would still contend that layouts done by hand are still better than those done with computer-aided design.[13] It is likely that considerations similar to the relative merits of hand coding and compiled code in software design also apply here. As mentioned above, silicon compilers and the like have started to appear and will presumably get better and better. But in the same way that hand coding is still necessary for the highest-performance software when cost is no object, then hand layouts may still have the edge for very demanding designs. If all this seems trivial, then one is reminded of the description 'real estate'; the technology is still not quite so good that space on the chip is free.[14]

We now turn to the relationship between functional design, capacity, and performance (speed). It was mentioned above that the maximum speed of elementary components depended on fundamental resolution, but that for any given resolution there were different performance characteristics for different types of transistor (MOS or bipolar), and that speed could—in a sense—be bought for higher power consumption. Different technologies offer different maximum speeds (see Chapter 4). For any given gate speed—or its inverse, gate delay—functional performance will naturally depend on the sequence of logical operations. In addition, the length of connecting leads may be important when a chip contains large synchronous networks; if an attempt is made to drive the chip too fast, the electrons will not be able to travel around the chip fast enough (see Hoenissen and Mead, 1972; Folberth and Bleher, 1979).

Finally, there is the relation between functional design, capacity, and power dissipation. There are two parts to power dissipation: static and dynamic. Any component will consume power even if it is not active in a logical sense; this is static power dissipation (W_s), rather like a fixed cost. In addition, components use extra power when they are logically active—recall that a logical operation involves the discharging of node capacitances (Section 3.3). The marginal or dynamic power dissipation is proportional to the rate of logical activity (clock speed). If the constant of proportionality is w_d and clock speed is C, then the total power dissipation is $W = W_s + w_d C$.

For any operation, the circuit's power dissipation is the sum of static dissipation for all gates and dynamic dissipation for all active gates. It is usual to quote a maximum power dissipation which is the maximum over all combinations of functional operation. Present packaging techniques, as mentioned above, can only cope with a maximum dissipation of one or two watts per chip, and this can act as a constraint on functional design and capacity.

Notes

1. The original equipment manufacturer (OEM) takes a system manufacturer's product and sells it under his own (OEM) name with perhaps a small amount of custom tailoring, often in software.
2. Noyce (1977) gives a neat explanation of why this should be.
3. For the new Inmos 'transputer', the building block is no longer the logic gate but the 'Occam' (Barron, 1984).
4. See Sutherland and Mead (1977). Software is not cheap, however, and for some sorts of application, semi-custom 'hard-wired' designs are appropriate.
5. The 'data flow' computer is an exception, but it is still very much at the development stage.
6. Without the impurities, silicon is a very indifferent conductor.
7. An alternative derivation is in terms of the Bose–Einstein Statistics; see Feller (1968, pp. 40ff).
8. $(1-f)^{nA} \simeq 1 - nfA - \ldots \simeq e^{-nfA}$
9. The argument here follows that in Cunningham and Jaffee (1975) and Wise *et al.* (1980).
10. $(c_1 m + c_2 d + T)/S = 0.0068$ \$/mm^2 of raw silicon; $P = \$0.45$; $f = 0.016$ mm^{-2}.
11. Yet the number of transistors is sometimes used as a measure of capacity, irrespective of regularity.
12. An explanation of this is given by Meindl (1977); for details on these different maximum densities, see Section 4.3.
13. An executive of one of Intel's rivals told me that Intel's layouts are without equal because they use *ad hoc* manual methods rather than computer-aided design.
14. But recall the remark of A. Grove, quoted at the beginning of Chapter 1.

4 Microelectronic Technology: A Brief Outline of Developments

In this chapter, we shall describe in broad outline the development of microelectronic technology over the past twenty years. Chapters 5 and 6 will then examine particular aspects of the history. In Chapter 2, we referred to maximum qualities: the highest quality of the good that could be produced at the current 'state of the art'. This chapter can be seen as an attempt to describe how the maximum qualities have increased over the period.

Section 4.1 describes some of the principal innovations of the period, and argues that the underlying process has been one of refinement rather than radical innovation. Section 4.2 explains some of the important summary parameters, and Section 4.3 describes the developments in those parameters. Section 4.4 tries to put these developments in perspective. We note that large expenditures on research and development have been needed to take advantage of the developments.

The data referred to in this chapter are obtained from a wide variety of sources, notably: *Electronics*, various issues, Verhofstadt (1976), Petritz (1978), Wilson *et al.* (1980), Noyce (1977), Noyce and Barrett (1979), Bloch and Henle (1968), Braun and MacDonald (1978), and Mayo (1977).[1] This chapter is necessarily rather brief. For further details, reference is made to the excellent studies by Dummer (1978), Tilton (1971), Sciberras (1977), Wilson *et al.* (1980), Wise *et al.* (1980), Webbink (1977), *inter alia.*

4.1 The principal innovations

Although the transistor was discovered in 1947 and devices were commercially available from 1951, it was the invention of the silicon transistor in 1954 that was crucial to the development of digital integrated electronics. The development of oxide masking and diffusion in 1956, followed by their refinement in the planar process (1960), paved the way for the integrated circuit in 1961.

Since then the basic techniques used in the manufacture of integrated circuits have not changed substantially. New varieties of process have appeared, and old processes have been refined; new products within the definition 'integrated circuit' have appeared, too, but the underlying techniques are the same.

The earliest transistors, made of germanium, were neither very fast nor—to begin with—very reliable. The silicon transistor was faster and could operate over a wider temperature range, and when the oxide masking and diffusion techniques were invented, these silicon transistors could be made very cheaply.

The integrated circuit was attractive mainly because it offered enormous cost reductions and reliability improvements. Transistors were reasonably fast, and more reliable than valves, but assembly costs for discrete components were considerable.

Early integrated circuits (1961) were made with technologies such as Direct Coupled Transistor Logic (DCTL) and Resistor Capacitor Transistor Logic (RCTL). The resulting devices were, however, rather slow, and these technologies were rapidly displaced by Resistor Transistor Logic (RTL) and Diode Transistor Logic (DTL), introduced in 1961 and 1962 respectively. These technologies were faster than DCTL and RCTL without consuming excessive power. But the most successful of the early bipolar technologies was Transistor Transistor Logic (TTL), introduced in 1964 and refined versions of which are still in use today. A speciality process called Emitter Coupled Logic (ECL) dating from 1962 has survived, too, mainly because as the fastest-known integrated circuit technology on silicon it is widely used in the construction of large computers.

The technologies that have been of greatest importance in the spread of digital integrated electronics are the Metal Oxide Silicon (MOS) technologies. The p-channel MOS (pMOS), the first MOS technology, dates back to about 1966. It is easy to manufacture, dense, and uses relatively little power compared to bipolar technologies. Its main drawback is its very slow speed, and it was not—in the mid-1960s—seen as a serious threat to TTL and ECL in large computers, which indeed it has not been. The pMOS technology was improved and used in the first generation of microprocessors, but it has now really been supplanted by the n-channel MOS (nMOS) which appeared in about 1971. This nMOS

A brief outline of developments

is much faster than pMOS without being that much more complex to make. Indeed, it is now as fast as most bipolar technologies, and cheaper to make. The third MOS technology (of those which have been widely used) is something of a curiosity; called Complementary MOS (CMOS), its distinguishing feature is its very low power consumption. Introduced in about 1968, it was written off by some observers because the elementary components took a lot of space ('real estate'), making CMOS rather expensive. Subsequently, however, it has proved invaluable for the manufacture of digital watches, pocket calculators, etc., and it can now match nMOS for speed and (nearly) for density.

4.2 The most important technology parameters

The most important parameters with which to describe developments in the technology are:

(a) power dissipation;
(b) maximum speed and minimum gate delay;
(c) the power-delay product;
(d) maximum component density;
(e) process complexity;
(f) component reliability.

In this section we outline exactly what is being measured.

(a) Power dissipation

As discussed above, there are two parts to power dissipation—static and dynamic—and consequently, great care must be taken when comparing the power dissipations of different technologies. The ranking of different technologies may depend on the work rate (clock speed) assumed. CMOS is very different from the others. It has negligible static power dissipation, but a fairly high dynamic dissipation, so that above about 1 MHz (10^6 Hz) it consumes more power than IIL (Integrated Injection Logic) and nMOS. To talk of a power dissipation for CMOS is then rather misleading but it is still done. For the other technologies, total power dissipation varies less over the frequency range. When a single power dissipation figure is quoted, it is usually that corresponding to the maximum clock speed. It is worth mentioning that considerable discrepancies exist in different people's estimates of these parameters.

(b) Maximum speed and minimum gate delay

The maximum clock speed at which a technology can operate is naturally inversely proportional to the time taken for an elementary component to switch on or off. As a rough rule of thumb,[2] the maximum clock speed is something like 1/(4 × Gate Delay), where clock speed is measured in Hertz, gate delay is in seconds, and the factor of four is included as a safety margin when complex logical operations in different parts of the circuit are slightly out of phase. Comparisons between technologies ought to be straightforward, but once again there are sizeable discrepancies between different people's estimates of the parameter.

(c) The power-delay product

This is simply the product of total power dissipation at the maximum speed and the minimum gate delay. As such it is the minimum total energy required for a single gate operation. This may be insufficient on its own, as the profile of energy consumption may be important, but it is still a useful measure.

(d) Maximum component density

The area of silicon required to build a logical gate is normally quoted in square mils (1 mil = 10^{-3} inches ≈ 0.025 mm), but sometimes it is measured in millimetres. Corresponding to this area is a maximum gate density, usually quoted in gates/mm². As we saw above, the maximum is not generally achieved because attainable topographical efficiency is usually something less than 100 per cent. It is important, then, to take care when interpreting data on gate densities; they could be maximum densities, or they could be the sort of densities that can typically be attained (Barron and Curnow, 1979, p. 70).

(e) Process complexity

As we saw above, manufacturing costs depend on process complexity, defined in terms of masking steps and diffusion (or implantation) steps. These two parameters do not completely describe complexity; semiconductor engineers suggest that some processes are, in a rather subtle way, more lenient than others. Nevertheless, these are the two most important parameters.

(f) Component reliability

The relevant parameter here is the mean number of failures per gate

**Gate power-delay
product (pJ)**

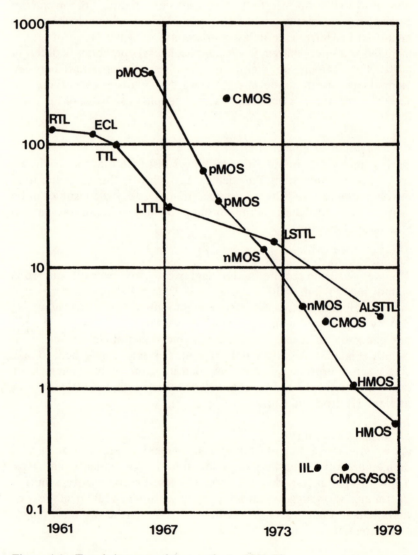

Figure 4.1 Trends in power-delay products, 1961–79

hour in the field. Sometimes the inverse, i.e. mean time between failure (mtbf) is quoted instead. It is important to note that reliability figures do not deal with devices that fail under test in the factory; those are taken care of in yield figures.

4.3 Developments in the technology parameters

Perhaps the most interesting starting-point is to look at the development of the power-delay product for digital integrated circuits. As there is in general a trade-off between low power dissipation and low gate delays, the power-delay product is a useful summary parameter. Moreover, as the amount of energy required for a logical operation, it has some intuitive meaning, too. It is usually quoted in picoJoules (10^{-12} Joules).

Figure 4.1 shows the power-delay product of different technologies arranged by approximate date of introduction.[3] The first point to notice is that the power-delay products of bipolar technologies and of MOS technologies have been falling steadily, but those of MOS have fallen faster. Secondly, two new and, as yet, not widely used technologies, IIL and CMOS/SOS have very low power-delay products, but these are being approached by HMOS, a refined version of nMOS.

The fall in the power-delay product is extremely important, a factor of about 1,000 from RCTL/DCTL in 1960 to HMOS II in 1979. The importance of this can perhaps best be judged by analogy. The inverse of the power-delay product, as the number of logical operations that can be done with a certain amount of energy, is rather like the miles-per-gallon measure for a car; 30 miles per gallon may not be all that good, but it is a vast improvement over 50–100 yards per gallon, or 3–4 refills per mile.

It is also informative to look at power dissipation and gate delay parameters separately. Figure 4.2 shows developments in power dissipation; bipolar technologies deriving from TTL are grouped into two categories, high speed on the one hand and low power on the other. ECL is a category on its own, as is CMOS, while pMOS and nMOS can be grouped together. The general picture is this: within any one of these groups, power dissipation has not changed much over the years, and attainable power dissipation has fallen more as a result of the appearance of new technologies.

With gate delays, the opposite is the case: in Figure 4.3 the technologies are grouped as before, but it is evident that within each group there

A brief outline of developments

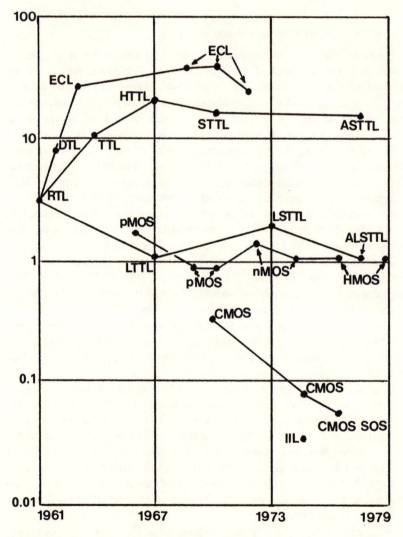

Figure 4.2 Trends in power dissipation, 1961–79

Gate delay (nS)

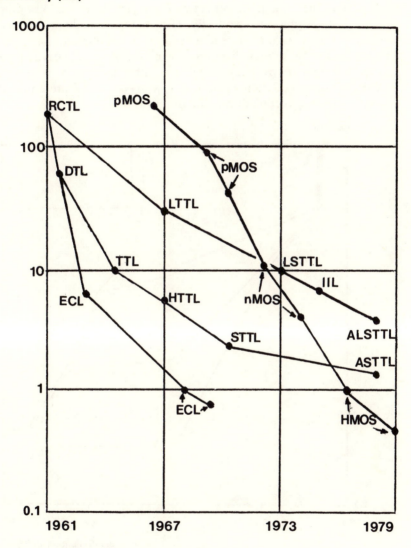

Figure 4.3 Trends in gate delays, 1961–79

A brief outline of developments

have been substantial reductions in gate delays, most notably in MOS. The newer technologies have, as it were, been catching up.

The microelectronics literature makes much use of diagrams like Figure 4.4. There the trade-off between low gate delays and low power consumption is presented explicitly. The cumulative undominated technologies[4] for any year are linked together with a continuous line, and in Figure 4.4 a series of these lines are drawn to represent the development of the technologies over time. They are rather like the rings in a tree trunk, or rather a quarter segment of it, with each ring representing the growth in each direction during the five previous years.

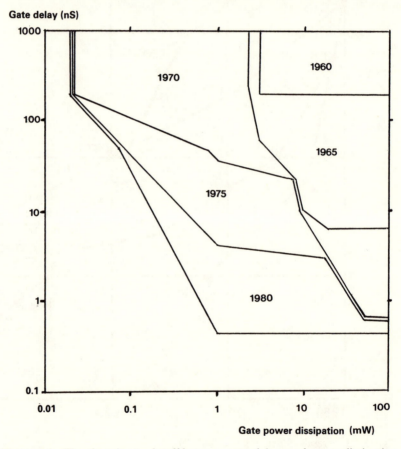

Figure 4.4 The changing trade-off between gate-delays and power dissipation, 1960–80

The pattern is reasonably clear. From 1960 to 1965 the development was mainly in faster technologies (TTL, ECL), while in 1965 to 1970 there were developments both in the faster technologies (ECL) and in low power technologies (pMOS,nMOS). From 1970 to 1975 the main development was in the middle-range technologies, with medium speed and medium to low power (such as nMOS and LSTTL). That trend has been continued to 1980 where, in addition, medium to low power technologies appear to match some high power technologies for speed.

Component density has for some time been used as a measure of the progress of microelectronics. The number of components per integrated circuit is widely quoted, too. This is not a measure of density exactly, because the number of components per chip can rise simply because the chip size has increased, and not as a result of further miniaturization. But as we saw above, there are sizeable packaging and cooling space overheads for each chip, so that the volume of the chip itself is small in proportion to the volume required to house a chip. Components per chip may, then, be a rather good measure of attainable density in the finished product.

There is a widely used rule of thumb known as Moore's Law,[5] which states that the number of components per chip doubles each year.[6] Petritz (1978) has gone further, and breaks this annual doubling into three parts: that part due to reductions in the elementary dimensions (line widths) used in lithography; that part due to improved chip topography or circuit and device 'cleverness'; and that part due to increases in chip size. He suggests that components per chip rose from 1 (2^0) in 1960 to 1,000,000 (2^{20}) in 1980, and of this factor of 2^{20}, a factor of 2^7 is due to reductions in elementary dimensions, a factor of 2^8 is due to improvements in topography (or cleverness), and 2^5 is due to increases in chip size.[7] In short, 2^{15} (or 70 per cent per annum) is due to pure increase in density.

Bloch and Henle (1968) projected similar trends, though they like to differentiate between circuits in development, circuits in production, and those circuits actually incorporated in finished machines. They suggest that circuits in advanced development may be some five years ahead of those which are just in production, and the latter may be a further five years ahead of those incorporated in finished machines—for more evidence on this, see Chapter 8.

So much for a rule of thumb. Ideally, we would present gate densities for each of the technologies identified before, but unfortunately the relevant data have proved very elusive or highly unreliable. The following figures derived from Verhofstadt (1976) give some idea of the maximum densities that can be achieved with different technologies, and represents the 'state of the art' in about 1976.

	(gates/mm^2)
IIL	400
CMOS/SOS	320
nMOS	270
pMOS	200
CMOS	160
STTL	80
ECL	80
TTL	40

If it is difficult to say much about the gate densities of different microelectronic technologies, then it is equally hard to say much about process complexity. A few general points can be made. In the mid-1960s, pMOS (the first MOS process) was much simpler to make than the bipolar technologies TTL and ECL. While the simplest pMOS process required only four mask steps and only one diffusion, bipolar processes could need as many as ten masks and four diffusions.[8] When nMOS appeared in about 1971, it was slightly more complex to make than pMOS, but still much simpler than the bipolar processes. CMOS, on the other hand, was of similar complexity to some of the bipolar processes.

In the 1970s, the main trend was the increasing complexity of nMOS and its refinements, while CMOS and the bipolar processes only became slightly more complex. According to *Electronics* (13 September 1979), in 1973 nMOS required between five and seven mask steps compared to between eight and nine for CMOS, but by 1980, nMOS and CMOS were of about equal complexity at eight to ten mask steps each.

The final parameter to be discussed is reliability. Noyce and Barrett (1979) suggest that reliability has increased by a factor of ten each four years between 1960 and 1980:

	Fails/gate hour
1960:	10^{-7}
1964:	10^{-8}
1968:	10^{-9}
1972:	10^{-10}
1976:	10^{-11}
1980:	10^{-12}

No evidence has been found of any substantial differences in reliability between the different technologies, except in how their reliability falls in a bad environment—see Chapter 8, and the discussion of electronics in cars. These figures can be assumed to hold approximately for all technologies, MOS or bipolar, in a good environment.

4.4 A perspective on the technology developments

The preceding discussion can be summarized quite well by comparing the 'order of magnitude' improvements in each technology parameter. These are presented in Table 4.1, which also gives a rough idea of the reduction in prices per gate over the same period. To help put these changes in perspective, an analogy is suggested for each parameter, similar to the miles-per-gallon analogy discussed above.[9] All of these order of magnitude improvements are dramatic, but improvements in density and reliability are the most dramatic.

It is interesting to compare these improvements with those experienced in the early years of other goods. A factor of 1,000 in twenty years represents a doubling of quality in two years, or a halving of price in two

Table 4.1 'Order of magnitude' improvements in some technology parameters, 1960–80

Parameter	Order of magnitude improvement	Analogy
Power delay product (pJ)	1,000	50 yards/gallon up to 30 miles/gallon
Power (mW)	1,000	A night store heater down to a dim torchlight
Delay (nS)	500	3 yards/minute up to 50 mph
Density (gates/chip) (gates/unit area)	10^5–10^6 10^4–10^5	4-drawer filing cabinet down to pocket calculator
Reliability (fails/hour)	10^5	1 fail each five minutes down to 1 fail each year
Price per gate	500	————

years. Results in Bain (1962) suggest that price reductions in the early days of television were not of this order. This is not surprising since the cost reductions that occur for microelectronic components would not apply for electron tubes. Nevertheless, some quality improvements were quite striking even if not comparable. Between 1953 and 1955, UK television broadcast hours rose from 35 hours per week to 50 hours per week. In 1950, all television sets had screens of 9 inches or less; by 1959, almost all were 17 inches or more. In the early days of car manufacture, prices dropped fairly rapidly. Bardon *et al.* (1983) note that the Ford Model T price fell from $900 in 1910 to $350 in 1917—nearly a factor of 3 in seven years. Over the period 1922–33, the price of bicycles fell by a factor of 3 (Derksen and Rombouts, 1937).

It should be noted, however, that while these developments are very striking, it has been an expensive business to exploit them. According to the *Business Week* R & D Scoreboard for 1979 (*Business Week*, 7 July 1980), the two industries with the highest ratios of research and development expenditures to sales are information processing (computers and peripherals) and semiconductors, with ratios of 6.1 per cent and 5.7 per cent respectively. Moreover, some of the companies in these industries spent rather more than the industry average. Thus, for example, Intel spent some 10.1 per cent of sales on research and development, National Semiconductor 9.4 per cent, Fairchild 9.3 per cent, Advanced Micro Devices 7.4 per cent, Mostek 7.3 per cent and Motorola 6.2 per cent (*Business Week*, 7 July 1980 and 2 July 1979). These companies are some of the most important producers of microprocessors (see Chapter 6).

In passing, we should mention that these data are not really appropriate for company comparisons since some of these manufacturers produce a much wider variety of products than simply microelectronic components, and some of those products may be much less R & D-intensive than microelectronic components. Accordingly, the specialized semiconductor manufacturer would be expected to spend a higher proportion of his sales on R & D.

In conclusion, we should add that developments in the hardware side of the technology are only part of the story. If many applications of microelectronics can be thought of as small computer systems, then developments in software are equally—if not more—important. This is, however, a vast topic in its own right, and we cannot do justice to it in this study.[10]

Notes

1. The data described the 'state of the art' in the American industry. In Europe, and until the mid-1970s in Japan, the 'state of the art' would typically be somewhat behind that in the United States. It should be noted that different sources frequently give widely differing estimates, and the estimates should therefore be treated with some caution; they may only be accurate to within a factor of two either way.
2. *Electronics*, August 1971, p. 38.
3. This is the date at which a circuit made with that technology was first introduced.
4. The cumulative set of technologies available in any year are all those technologies introduced during or before that year. The undominated technologies are all those for which there is no other technology that is (in this context) both faster and consumes less power.
5. After G. Moore, now of Intel, though when he proposed it, of Fairchild.
6. It is now generally reckoned that this law broke down in about 1975, and thereafter the number of components per chip has doubled every two years. Barron, however, considers that the law can still be made to hold if wiring is included in the device count: see *Microprocessors and Microsystems*, October 1981, p. 367.
7. The first microprocessor (4004) was a chip of roughly 10 mm^2, while one of the most sophisticated microprocessors of 1981 (68000) is a chip of roughly 45 mm^2. This is approximately consistent with Petritz's observation.
8. *Electronics*, 20 February 1967, pp. 179ff.
9. No figure is presented for process complexity since processes have become more rather than less complex.
10. Swann (1983) describes some of these developments to 1980.

5 A Time Series of Price Functions For Microprocessors

We saw in Chapter 2 that where standard demand analysis uses a time series of prices, the analysis of quality and quantity choice requires a time series of price functions, relating price to quality. In this chapter we estimate a time series of price functions using data on sixty microprocessors over the period 1974–83. Price data come from *EDN Annual Surveys;* data on characteristics come from a variety of sources, for example Osborne and Kane (1981), Bursky (1978), *EDN, Electronics, Microprocessors and Microsystems.*[1]

In Section 5.1, we see that a simple graphical analysis of the price data gives some very useful hints about what we should expect the time series of functions to look like. Typically, manufacturers introduce their products at a fairly high price, and then reduce the price quite rapidly. With the continual introduction of improved qualities, the overall pattern is one of steady price reductions, and a falling premium for quality.

Section 5.2 briefly discusses some preliminaries to estimation. It might be thought that all problems of interest in the estimation of price functions had been solved long ago. It is one thing, however, to estimate a single price function as a local approximation; it is quite another to estimate a series of functions which gives an accurate representation of change over time. It is argued that the best method is to estimate a frontier price function, and following Horsley and Swann (1983) we shall estimate this from the 'undominated' products—those that cannot be bettered, or only at a higher price.

Then, in Section 5.3, we present estimates based on a function with twelve characteristics. For each year taken on its own, these estimates are by and large quite sensible. Nevertheless, when viewed as a time series, the price functions are not so satisfactory, in particular because the estimated parameters show an unexpected and unrealistic instability over time. We examine the possibility that this may be a result of the combination of multicollinearity and measurement errors, broadly interpreted, to include errors arising because some of the characteristics used are poor measures of quality.

Reducing the parameter space can often reduce multicollinearity, but at the same time it introduces the equally serious (if not worse) problem of specification error. We argue in Section 5.4, however, that the reduced dimension price function can be justified as the relevant price function for those concerned with a subset of characteristics, and find that the estimates of the reduced dimension function are rather more reliable.

In Section 5.5, we examine some scatter diagrams of the partial relationship between price and characteristics, and find some useful insights about why the larger dimension functions show some instability.

5.1 A graphical examination of price trends

A preliminary graphical examination of the price data will be useful. Figure 5.1 shows how the prices of Intel's microprocessors have moved over the period 1974–83. The prices quoted are American prices, in current dollars. For the purposes of clarity, the graph does not show all their products, but does show the most important.

Intel have been recognized as the market leaders in microprocessors—we shall have more to say on this in Chapter 6. In this sense, their pricing strategy is of particular interest. Their 8080 (an 8-bit microprocessor) is a good example: it was introduced in 1974 at a relatively high price, the price fell very rapidly to begin with, more gradually thereafter, and reached a floor of $4 in 1980. A similar trend is observed for most of their other products.

The graph also gives an indication of the premium for quality. The 8086, for example, is a 16-bit microprocessor, a great deal more powerful than the 8080. In 1978, the 8086 was nearly twenty times the price of the 8080; in 1983, the 8086 is about six times the price of the 8080. In the same way, the iAPX 432 (a 32-bit microprocessor) is currently a great deal more expensive than the 16-bit devices, but the premium is likely to fall in the next few years.

The pricing strategies of most other manufacturers are very similar to that of Intel, and call for no further comment. There is one exception, Texas Instruments: for many of their products, the price reductions between introduction and maturity are not nearly so marked. The reason for this is discussed in Sciberras (1977): essentially it is because they tend to introduce products at prices below cost to build up demand

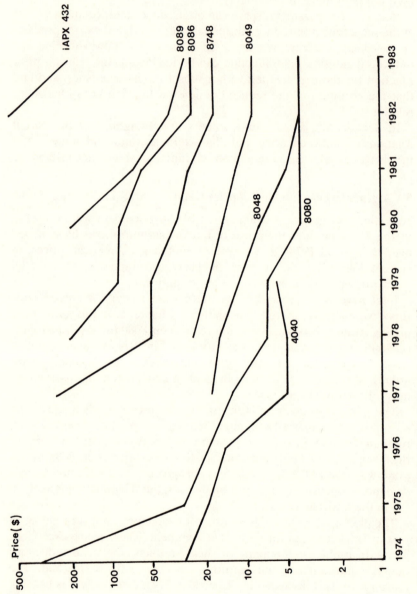

Figure 5.1   Prices of Intel microprocessors, 1974–83

as fast as possible in expectation of cost reductions as they move down the learning curve.

In summary, it would appear that a minimal requirement of any time series of price functions is that the prices of all qualities fall over time, and we would also expect the quality premium to fall over time. This is, of course, exactly what was predicted by the simple model of costs in Chapter 3.

5.2 Some preliminaries to estimation

There are three issues that must be discussed before estimation.[2] The first is the question of an appropriate functional form for the price functions. Secondly, the price data are quotes for particular quantities; in some cases they include (sizeable) quantity discounts, but in other cases they do not. Thirdly, there is evidence (see Horsley and Swann, 1983) that OLS (ordinary least squares regression) applied to the complete set of products is not an altogether satisfactory method for estimating price functions.

The form of the price function

We saw in Chapter 2 that the shape of the price function would not necessarily reflect the shape of consumer indifference curves or the best practice cost function. Rosen (1974) has shown that, with perfectly competitive buyers and sellers, price functions for the range of qualities traded could be interpreted as an envelope of both the consumers' indifference curves and the producers' cost functions. In a competitive market, this result would be very helpful in suggesting a suitable form for the price function. The envelope of producers' cost functions is simply the best practice cost function, and an appropriate functional form for this will also be an appropriate form for the price function. Moreover, we have seen in Chapter 3 that the best practice cost function can be described quite simply.

Competitiveness is crucial to this result, however, and while the microelectronics industry is certainly 'competitive', it is not perfectly competitive. Nevertheless, for the range of qualities traded, the price function must lie somewhere above the best practice cost function. Even though the functional forms will not necessarily be the same, our knowledge of the cost function does give us some idea about the form of the price function.

The model of Chapter 3 suggested that (before taking account of packaging) cost was proportional to the product of chip area and an exponential function of chip area (equation 3.2). Cost could also be written as a function of the number of gates (equation 3.4). Unfortunately, attempts to assemble data on chip areas and gates met with limited success, partly because many manufacturers do not publish such data, but also because they keep changing as manufacturers continue to make small modifications to their products. For that reason, we are obliged to work with a set of 'functional' specifications for each product.

The discussion of Section 3.6 does, however, suggest that chip area is simply the sum of the areas taken by the various functions on the chip. Thus, describing the specifications by z, and the corresponding parameters in the cost function by b, we obtain:

$$c = c_0 b'z \, e^{nfb'z} \qquad (5.1)$$

or taking logs:

$$\ln c = \ln c_0 + \ln(b'z) + nfb'z \qquad (5.2)$$

Such functions are rather inconvenient to estimate by regression methods, not simply because of the non-linearity, but also because the parameters b come into the function in two places. In any case, there is no certainty that the price function will have the same form as this cost function. For that reason, we have chosen to approximate the function (5.2).

As a practical matter, the question is really whether for the range of available qualities the proportional effect of chip area on cost dominates the exponential effect, or vice versa. If the former, we estimate (5.1) assuming that the exponential term is constant, and if the latter, we estimate (5.2) assuming that the term $\ln(b'z)$ is constant. In view of the discussion in Section 3.5 (especially Figure 3.3), our observations in the last section, and the typically low yields of working chips, we consider that the exponential effect dominates.

To a first order of approximation, therefore, we assume that price is an exponential function of the various microprocessor specifications, and accordingly estimate a semilog price function, $\ln p = $ constant $ + b'z$. With one exception—see below—we assume that the other specifications which do not represent chip area (add time, and the pMOS, CMOS and Bipolar dummies) affect price in the same manner. We use the Durbin–Watson statistic as a test for functional form, and find no evidence to reject this approximation.

Price functions with quantity discounts

The price quotes obtained for some products were for 'one-off' orders, while for other products the quotes were for very large volume orders (100,000). It is to be expected that large quantity discounts apply for such volumes. Manufacturers are evidently reluctant to quote one price for their products. From one point of view this is a mild nuisance, but it can also be seen as an indication of the manufacturers' wish to avoid price competition, and their dependence on price discrimination.

This is dealt with by simply assuming that there is a constant proportional quantity discount: thus, $-\mathrm{d}\ln p/\mathrm{d}\ln x = k$. Then it is simply a matter of including a term in $\ln x$ in the log price function. The results of Section 5.3 suggest that the value of k is in the region of 20 per cent.

Estimation with undominated points

Horsley and Swann (1983) estimated a time series of price functions for mainframe computers,[3] using the data gathered by Knight (1966). The great virtue of these data is that performance is reduced to a scalar measure, thus making graphical examination possible. It was found that if the estimate of the price function in any year was based on the set of machines introduced in that year, the series of functions obtained was not altogether satisfactory. It was observed that a large number of machines were inefficient in the sense that there was a cheaper machine offering equal or even higher performance, and it was suggested that what we are really interested in is the efficient price function rather than the average price function. Moreover, it was found that it is better to base the price function for any year on the set of machines available in that year, not just on the machines introduced in the year.

The question is, however, what is the best method of estimation which would give particular attention to the efficient products and less attention to the inefficient? There seem to be four possibilities. The first is to let a product drop out of the efficient set after some fixed time, but this is not really satisfactory as some products become outdated faster than others.

The second is to weight the observations by the sales of that product in the year. This neat idea has been used to good effect in studies estimating price functions—for example, Cowling and Rayner (1970). One practical problem here is that data on sales of individual products are often hard to come by, and simply not available in long runs. There are two further theoretical difficulties with this method. First, a product may sell well because of some unmeasured characteristic—brand loyalty, for example—and not because it is a particularly good bargain as a source of the characteristics that are actually measured. Second, it may give more weight to low quality products than to high quality products—simply because more low quality products are bought—and thus put too little weight on efficient high quality products.

The third approach is to fit the function to the complete set of products, but to use some form of asymmetric error weighting—this is rather like the estimation of frontier production functions (Schmidt, 1976; Aigner *et al.* 1977). Many procedures for estimation with non-normal errors have been suggested, but the problem with many of them—the half normal, for example—is that they give outlying points disproportionate and misleading weight.

The fourth, and we would argue best, procedure is to select those products which are not dominated by another product; a product can be said to dominate another if it offers equal quality for lower cost, or if it offers greater quality for the same cost. These are, after all, the points that would be of interest in a discrete choice analysis.

While we do not do so in this study, it could also be useful to extract the convex hull; the convex hull is of course a subset of the set of undominated points, for any point in the convex hull is not merely undominated by any other product, but also undominated by any convex combination of other products. Farrell (1957) pioneered the use of the convex hull of productive units in the measurement of productive efficiency and in some cases the same technique can be very useful for the measurement of product competitiveness (see Swann, 1984, 1985b, 1985c).

5.3 A large dimension price function

Table 5.1 presents the estimates of a time series of price functions estimated from the undominated microprocessors amongst the set of sixty for which sufficient data were available.[4] Twelve characteristics were measured,[5] though four of them form an exhaustive set of dummies so that only eleven characteristics were included in the regressions.

Table 5.1 Price function estimates (large dimension price function), 1975–83

1975

i	1	2	3	4	5	6	7	8	9	10	11	12	13	
b_i	3.3	-0.081	0.054	-0.009	1.2	1.05	0.036	-0.19	0.019	-0.035	0.38	0.73	—	$R^2=0.996$
SE	1.6	0.12	0.17	0.021	2.1	2.2	1.2	0.13	0.054	0.055	0.84	0.63	—	DW=2.18
HCSE	0.62	0.051	0.058	0.0054	0.60	1.4	0.47	0.023	0.014	0.018	0.19	0.22	—	ESE=0.49
CLME	0.28	3.7	2.6	21	0.21	0.20	0.20	0.37	8.1	7.9	0.52	0.69	—	$N=17$ $N^*=16$

1976

i	1	2	3	4	5	6	7	8	9	10	11	12	13	
b_i	1.3	-0.002	0.19	0.007	-0.35	0.59	-0.81	-0.019	-0.003	-0.001	0.12	0.30	—	$R^2=0.988$
SE	1.6	0.11	0.15	0.015	1.7	2.1	0.80	0.081	0.027	0.016	0.36	0.42	—	DW=2.08
HCSE	1.1	0.081	0.12	0.010	1.2	1.6	0.44	0.053	0.015	0.008	0.18	0.38	—	ESE=0.51
CLME	0.20	2.7	2.1	21	0.18	0.15	0.38	3.8	11	19	0.86	0.73	—	$N=25$ $N^*=22$

1977

i	1	2	3	4	5	6	7	8	9	10	11	12	13	
b_i	3.8	-0.26	-0.067	-0.18	2.7	1.8	-0.035	-0.043	0.045	-0.015	0.31	-0.15	2.2	$R^2=0.990$
SE	0.67	0.076	0.063	0.008	0.89	1.5	0.44	0.046	0.019	0.012	0.28	0.31	0.37	DW=2.03
HCSE	0.50	0.044	0.041	0.0052	0.55	0.94	0.34	0.044	0.016	0.008	0.18	0.13	0.23	ESE=0.42
CLME	0.32	2.8	3.4	27	0.24	0.15	0.49	4.7	12	18	0.78	0.69	0.58	$N=31$ $N^*=27$

1978

i	1	2	3	4	5	6	7	8	9	10	11	12	13	
b_i	3.3	-0.22	-0.041	-0.013	2.3	-0.72	0.098	0.037	0.008	-0.003	0.28	0.21	1.9	$R^2=0.989$
SE	0.47	0.030	0.043	0.005	0.54	1.1	0.35	0.015	0.009	0.010	0.22	0.27	0.34	DW=2.12
HCSE	0.42	0.023	0.033	0.005	0.49	0.91	0.19	0.010	0.006	0.008	0.19	0.23	0.20	ESE=0.38
CLME	0.32	5.0	3.5	28	0.28	0.14	0.44	10	17	15	0.69	0.55	0.45	$N=42$ $N^*=37$

Table 5.1 (continued)

1979

i	1	2	3	4	5	6	7	8	9	10	11	12	13	
b_i	2.4	-0.21	-0.11	-0.010	2.1	1.8	0.36	0.037	0.011	0.002	0.59	-0.30	2.1	R^2=0.981
SE	0.61	0.035	0.056	0.007	0.73	1.0	0.41	0.017	0.013	0.014	0.33	0.37	0.45	DW=2.07
HCSE	0.64	0.042	0.049	0.0067	0.70	0.83	0.29	0.011	0.0067	0.0098	0.27	0.21	0.24	ESE=0.52
CLME	0.32	5.5	3.5	27	0.27	0.19	0.48	11	16	14	0.59	0.52	0.43	N=47 N^*=40

1980

i	1	2	3	4	5	6	7	8	9	10	11	12	13	
b_i	1.7	-0.25	0.082	0.006	0.41	1.8	0.35	0.026	0.030	0.005	0.37	0.55	1.9	R^2=0.965
SE	0.87	0.063	0.081	0.008	1.0	1.4	0.47	0.017	0.017	0.020	0.50	0.41	0.58	DW=1.95
HCSE	0.86	0.035	0.077	0.009	1.0	1.3	0.28	0.008	0.008	0.008	0.21	0.66	0.55	ESE=0.64
CLME	0.27	3.8	3.0	29	0.23	0.17	0.51	14	14	12	0.47	0.58	0.41	N=49 N^*=41

1981

i	1	2	3	4	5	6	7	8	9	10	11	12	13	
b_i	-0.76	-0.14	0.30	0.023	-2.0	1.9	0.098	0.025	0.017	0.024	0.22	0.041	1.8	R^2=0.966
SE	1.1	0.067	0.10	0.011	1.2	1.4	0.45	0.016	0.016	0.052	0.53	0.50	0.60	DW=1.87
HCSE	0.82	0.045	0.091	0.0065	0.84	1.6	0.35	0.0091	0.011	0.042	0.33	0.56	0.67	ESE=0.59
CLME	0.21	3.6	2.3	23	0.20	0.17	0.53	15	15	4.6	0.45	0.48	0.40	N=44 N^*=36

1982

i	1	2	3	4	5	6	7	8	9	10	11	12	13	
b_i	-0.74	-0.18	0.33	0.02	-1.8	1.2	-0.02	0.034	0.014	0.028	0.45	0.094	1.4	R^2=0.960
SE	1.4	0.080	0.12	0.012	1.4	1.6	0.54	0.019	0.019	0.060	0.61	0.57	0.68	DW=1.70
HCSE	1.2	0.064	1.2	0.010	1.2	1.4	0.40	0.008	0.012	0.045	0.40	0.58	0.68	ESE=0.67
CLME	0.20	3.5	2.3	23	0.20	0.17	0.51	15	15	4.6	0.46	0.49	0.41	N=43 N^*=35

1983

i	1	2	3	4	5	6	7	8	9	10	11	12	13	
b_i	-0.29	-0.18	0.19	0.014	-0.62	1.7	0.21	0.026	0.019	0.092	-0.051	-0.48	2.1	$R^2 = 0.963$
SE	1.2	0.073	0.11	0.011	1.2	1.6	0.50	0.016	0.018	0.056	0.55	0.66	0.68	DW = 2.07
HCSE	0.88	0.049	0.083	0.008	0.90	0.95	0.28	0.011	0.010	0.024	0.32	0.33	0.54	ESE = 0.58
CLME	0.21	3.5	2.2	23	0.20	0.16	0.51	16	14	4.5	0.46	0.38	0.37	$N = 41$ $N^* = 33$

HCSE = Heteroscedasticity-consistent standard error
CLME = Critical level of measurement error
N = Total number of observations
N^* = Number of undominated observations
DW = Durbin–Watson statistic
ESE = Equation standard error

In addition, the regressions include the log quantity term (as discussed in the last section) and a constant. The variables are numbered as follows:

(1) constant;
(2) log quantity;
(3) bit size: the number of bits of information on which the processor can operate at any one time;
(4) number of instructions: a rough measure of the processing power of the microprocessor;
(5) instruction content: an estimate of the size of the instruction memory (Kilobits);[6]
(6) registers: a measure of the processing flexibility of the micropro-cessor (Kilobits);
(7) Random Access Memory (RAM): this is the read-and-write memory used in any small computer system;
(8) Read Only Memory (ROM): this is the (user-defined) program memory (Kilobits);
(9) Input/Output ports (I/O): these are the lines by which the micro-computer communicates with external devices;
(10) add time: this is the time taken by the processor to add two numbers of n bits, where n is the bit size (time measured in microseconds);
(11) pMOS dummy
(12) CMOS dummy   (all other devices are nMOS)
(13) Bipolar dummy

As described in the last section, the functions are semilog; they are estimated by OLS using the undominated products in any period. As defined, characteristics (3)–(9) are 'good', and (10) is bad, while (11)–(13) are ambiguous. Thus one product (A) is deemed (weakly) to dominate another (B) if all of the following are true: A has an equal or lower price than B, for an equal or smaller order; A has an equal or greater value for (3)–(9) than B; A has an equal or lower value for (10) than B. Strong dominance is defined in an obvious manner. Character-istics (11)–(13) are ignored in the calculation of undominated products.

The results

Table 5.1 presents conventional and heteroscedasticity-consistent stan-dard errors (White, 1980). It is interesting to observe that these two do not differ by a great deal, though the heteroscedasticity consistent estimate is often about a half of the conventional estimate. For two reasons the calculated standard errors may be unduly pessimistic. Firstly, if the observations represent an almost complete survey of all available products, then at least as far as the consumer is concerned, almost the entire population is to hand, and there can be little or no sampling variation in the parameter estimates. We do not propose, however, to calculate appropriate measures for sampling from a finite and small population.

Secondly, the quoted parameter standard errors are calculated on the (implicit) assumption that only the undominated points provide information which helps in locating the price functions. But there can be no doubt that the dominated points, even if excluded from the set of points used to estimate the price function, still contribute some information towards locating the efficient price function. For want of a systematic method of adjusting the quoted (heteroscedasticity-consistent) standard errors for this additional information, the standard errors are quoted unadjusted, but they may well be too high.

Table 5.1 also quotes the Durbin–Watson statistic for each regression, where products are ordered in terms of price. The statistic can be interpreted in this context as a test that the chosen functional form is appropriate. Positive autocorrelation would be interpreted as evidence that the function has excessive or insufficient curvature.[7] The Durbin–Watson statistics for these regressions are all between 1.7 and 2.2, which suggests that the semilog form is satisfactory.

The equation standard errors are in the region of 0.5, which is rather high, given that the dependent variable is in (natural) logs. Nevertheless, in view of the fact that many manufacturers quote very wide ranges for their prices, we should not be too concerned. Of greater concern, perhaps, are the parameter standard errors. In many cases these are rather large, so that a 95 per cent confidence interval straddles zero.[8] The estimates are not a bad starting-point, however; taking any year on its own, it seems likely that with some refinement, sensible parameter estimates could be obtained.

For the purposes of this study, we are particularly interested in the functions as a time series. Figure 5.2 plots four of the estimated coefficients as a time series.[9] From this point of view, the estimates are not satisfactory. They show unexpected and unlikely instability, which in some cases obscures any trend. In some cases there appears to be an upward trend in the coefficient; this is contrary to our expectation, but

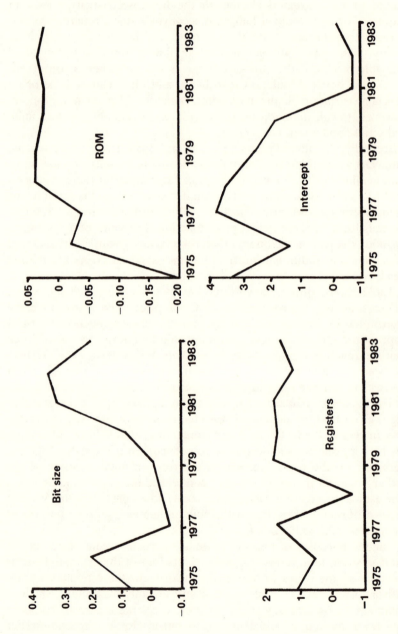

Figure 5.2 Time series of price function coefficients (large dimension price function)

would be an interesting finding if we could trust our estimates. The emphasis, then, should be on trying to improve our estimates as a time series.

Multicollinearity and measurement errors

It is possible that some of the unreliability in the estimates is attributable to measurement error. As demonstrated in Swann (1982), measurement error bias is exacerbated by multicollinearity. We saw in Chapter 3 that there was reason to expect technology parameters to be interrelated, and our knowledge of the data confirms that there is likely to be some multicollinearity.

While the specifications of the microprocessors are measured without error in the sense that they have been copied down correctly from the product data books, they are at best rather imperfect measures of quality. To investigate the possible importance of measurement error bias, we make use of a diagnostic for the critical level of measurement error (Swann, 1982).

First, the partial variance of each regressor (independent of the others) can be interpreted as a critical level of random measurement error for that regressor. If measurement error accounts for a large proportion of the measured partial variance, then the measurement error bias will be very serious.

Table 5.1 presents the critical levels of measurement error (CLME), expressing them as two (partial) standard deviations of the explanatory variable: when we say that a particular observation is accurate to + or − 'e', then e could reasonably be interpreted as two standard deviations of measurement error. At first sight, these critical levels look reassuringly high. Thus the critical level of measurement error in bit size (3) is between 2 and 3.5 bits. Admittedly, bit size is not a perfect measure of quality, and for a few devices it is difficult to know whether to classify them as 8 or 16 bits. Nevertheless, this level of measurement error would seem to imply that we cannot in general distinguish between the 4- and the 8-bit device; that is certainly not true.

In the same way, the critical level for registers (6) is in the region of 0.15 to 0.2 Kilobits. The number and size of registers is not a perfect measure of processor flexibility: some very powerful and flexible processors have only a small number of registers, while some modest processors have a large number of registers. Nevertheless, measurement errors of this magnitude would seem to imply that we cannot really distinguish between the modest processors (0.1 register Kilobits) and the minicomputer processors (0.4 register Kilobits). Again, this is simply not so.

For most of the variables, the critical levels of measurement error seem to be well above the likely measurement error. There is one important exception: instructions (4). It is well known that this is a rather imperfect measure. Some manufacturers simply count the basic instructions, while stressing that there are many derivatives of the instructions; others count some of the derivatives. In the data collected for this study, we have counted only the basic instructions. Nevertheless, the same number of basic instructions may imply a widely differing number of derivative instructions. The critical level of about 20 instructions is not particularly high. For example, it is inconceivable that the PPS8 with 109 instructions is really more powerful than the 68000 with 78.

With highly collinear regressors, it only takes one variable to be measured with error to introduce measurement error bias. The question is, then, how collinear are the regressors? Inspection of the regressor covariance matrix, the matrix of partial correlation coefficients, and the matrix of subsidiary regression coefficients for regressions of one explanatory variable on another suggests that bit size, instructions and instruction content are very collinear, as are RAM, ROM and I/O.[10] The first observation is not surprising; the second is a consequence of clustering in product design—see Chapter 6. This suggests that measurement error could be at the root of the instability in the regression estimates.

5.4 A small dimension price function

If, as the last section suggests is possible, the time series of price functions shows instability because of multicollinearity and measurement error, then there could be a case for estimating a price function of rather smaller dimensions. Indiscriminately reducing the dimensions could, however, lead to specification bias, and indeed the greater the multicollinearity in a large dimension function, the greater the danger of specification bias in a reduced dimension function. Moreover, as Davidson *et al.* (1978) have argued, a mis-specified equation will show signs of instability when the correlation structure of the omitted variables changes, even though the 'true' relationship is not unstable. What we may gain on the swings we may lose on the roundabouts. Inspection of

Table 5.2 Price function estimates (small dimension price function), 1974–83

		1974				
i	1	2	3	6	8	
b_i	4.8	−0.27	−0.029	7.8	0.070	$R^2=0.996$
SE	1.0	0.096	0.062	3.7	0.073	DW=1.60
HCSE	0.48	0.043	0.024	2.6	0.025	ESE=0.45
CLME	0.44	4.7	7.2	0.12	6.2	$N=9\,N^*=8$

		1975				
i	1	2	3	6	8	
b_i	2.1	−0.027	0.12	3.8	−0.11	$R^2=1.000$
SE	0.16	0.021	0.014	0.64	0.023	DW=1.92
HCSE	0.077	0.016	0.010	0.36	0.016	ESE=0.11
CLME	0.66	4.8	7.0	0.16	4.4	$N=17\,N^*=9$

		1976				
i	1	2	3	6	8	
b_i	1.7	−0.069	0.12	3.7	0.019	$R^2=0.991$
SE	0.51	0.062	0.037	1.51	0.043	DW=1.63
HCSE	0.27	0.040	0.025	0.85	0.040	ESE=0.37
CLME	0.51	4.2	7.1	0.17	6.1	$N=25\,N^*=12$

		1977				
i	1	2	3	6	8	
b_i	2.4	−0.19	0.098	1.7	0.047	$R^2=0.979$
SE	0.68	0.083	0.048	1.9	0.036	DW=1.67
HCSE	0.57	0.066	0.032	1.3	0.030	ESE=0.45
CLME	0.44	3.6	6.3	0.16	8.3	$N=31\,N^*=13$

		1978				
i	1	2	3	6	8	
b_i	2.3	−0.24	0.10	2.1	0.057	$R^2=0.989$
SE	0.30	0.026	0.023	1.0	0.010	DW=2.28
HCSE	0.24	0.019	0.019	0.98	0.006	ESE=0.33
CLME	0.55	6.3	7.2	0.16	17	$N=42\,N^*=20$

Continued overleaf

Table 5.2 *(continued)*

1979

i	1	2	3	6	8	
b_i	1.7	−0.19	0.13	3.1	0.061	$R^2=0.978$
SE	0.33	0.033	0.025	0.93	0.013	DW=2.20
HCSE	0.37	0.038	0.019	0.69	0.008	ESE=0.48
CLME	0.65	6.5	8.4	0.23	16	$N=47\ N^*=24$

1980

i	1	2	3	6	8	
b_i	2.9	−0.29	0.087	1.4	0.073	$R^2=0.964$
SE	0.70	0.059	0.040	1.2	0.015	DW=1.97
HCSE	0.73	0.059	0.028	0.97	0.014	ESE=0.57
CLME	0.37	4.4	6.5	0.21	17	$N=49\ N^*=23$

1981

i	1	2	3	6	8	
b_i	0.77	−0.12	0.10	3.6	0.070	$R^2=0.951$
SE	0.84	0.070	0.047	1.7	0.018	DW=1.97
HCSE	0.52	0.050	0.023	1.2	0.011	ESE=0.57
CLME	0.36	4.4	6.4	0.18	17	$N=44\ N^*=18$

1982

i	1	2	3	6	8	
b_i	0.58	−0.15	0.14	3.7	0.077	$R^2=0.952$
SE	0.92	0.074	0.054	1.8	0.020	DW=1.47
HCSE	0.49	0.045	0.032	0.85	0.011	ESE=0.62
CLME	0.36	4.4	6.1	0.18	17	$N=43\ N^*=18$

1983

i	1	2	3	6	8	
b_i	1.1	−0.16	0.13	1.1	0.060	$R^2=0.953$
SE	0.82	0.066	0.047	1.5	0.017	DW=1.80
HCSE	0.38	0.034	0.018	0.58	0.012	ESE=0.51
CLME	0.36	4.5	6.3	0.20	18	$N=41\ N^*=16$

HCSE=Heteroscedasticity-consistent standard error
CLME=Critical level of measurement error
N=Total number of observations
N^*=Number of undominated observations
DW=Durbin–Watson statistic
ESE=Equation standard error

Table 5.1 suggests that it will be difficult to find zero restrictions on parameters that are acceptable in all periods.

There is, however, an alternative rationale for a reduced dimension function. Consider the user who is concerned only with a subset of the characteristics, and places no value on the others. He is concerned simply with the products that provide those characteristics cheaply; the appropriate function for him is one estimated from the products that are undominated in this subspace. From some perspective this price function may be inaccurate, but for this user it is the correct price function.

For that reason we present in Table 5.2 estimates of price functions with five parameters: the intercept (1), the log of quantity (2), bits (3), registers (6) and ROM (8). It is unlikely that there are many users for whom these are the only relevant characteristics, but then most users would be concerned with more than the dozen used in the last section. In any case, this subset should serve as an example to see if estimated small dimension price functions are more reliable.

As we suggested above, these reduced dimension functions are very unlikely to be acceptable as restricted forms of the equations in Table 5.1, but from this alternative perspective that does not really matter. A test is complicated since the procedure of taking undominated points changes the size of samples used for estimation. In Table 5.1, a fairly small number of products were dominated, so that most of the products were used in estimation; here, however, many more products are dominated—in later years, indeed, the majority.

The equation standard errors for these equations are (with one exception) rather smaller than those in Table 5.1: this is a result of the smaller samples used for estimation. The Durbin–Watson statistics are in some cases slightly worse than before, but the lowest is only 1.47. A preliminary glance at the coefficient estimates finds only two estimates of the 'wrong sign', and standard errors (both conventional and heteroscedasticity-consistent) are not surprisingly rather lower than those in Table 5.1. Likewise, critical levels of measurement error are in general somewhat higher.

Figure 5.3 plots the same four estimated coefficients (1, 3, 6, 8) as a time series. The estimates for 1974 are clearly rather unreliable; otherwise the time series are perhaps a little more believable than those in Figure 5.2, but not all that much. We would still be rather reluctant to use these in quality and quantity demand analysis.[11]

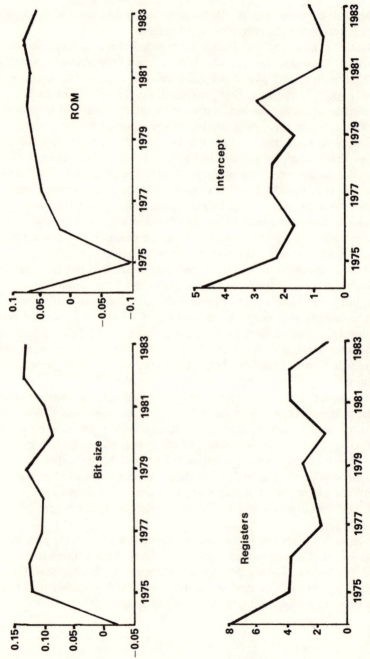

Figure 5.3 Time series of price function coefficients (small dimension price function)

5.5 Simple price-undominated quality relationships

We could take the argument of the previous section to its logical conclusion. Suppose there is a user who is concerned with one characteristic only; what is the appropriate function for him? The same argument as before suggests that the relevant products as far as this consumer is concerned are those which are undominated as a source of this characteristic; the price function should be estimated from the

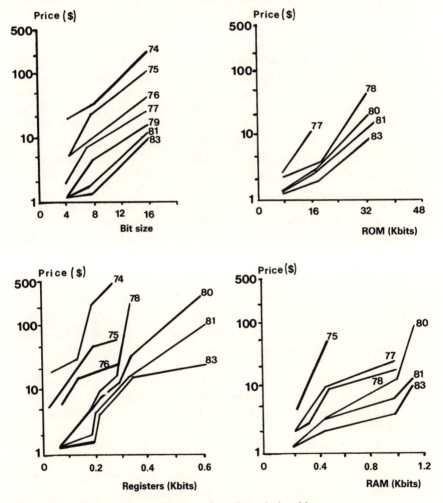

Figure 5.4 Simple price-undominated quality relationships

undominated points in that subspace. Again, there will be few such users, but a graphical examination of these simple relationships will be useful: the time series estimates obtained in previous sections were not altogether satisfactory, and the simple relationships suggest why.

Figure 5.4 shows the simple relationship between price (no adjustment is made for the order size to which the price refers) and quality for four characteristics, bits (3), registers (6), RAM (7), and ROM (8). The lines join together the undominated points. For the purposes of clarity, the lines for some years have been omitted; the longest gap, however, is only two years.

As expected, the lines progress downward and to the right over time. In some cases—bits in particular—the shape of the line does not change very much. In other cases—notably registers—the shape changes from convex to concave. Since the price axis is on a log scale, the semilog function would be trying to fit a straight line to the points as drawn. Taking registers as an example, it is clear that in some sense the marginal price of a register at a large number of registers has fallen between 1976 and 1978—from a notional infinite price. Nevertheless, a line fitted to the 1978 points would be steeper than one fitted to the 1976 points.

The nature of quality innovation is such that it is not easily described by changes in the slope and intercept of a semilog price function. A quadratic function might be an improvement, but even then there could be difficulties—for an example, see Horsley and Swann (1983).

Notes

1. For each product, the *EDN Survey* publishes a price per unit for a particular size of order. Typically, the order sizes used for microprocessors are much smaller than those used for single-chip microcomputers. In some cases, a fairly wide range of prices may be quoted, even for a particular size of order; it is a general problem with such surveys that manufacturers are usually reluctant to quote a single price. In such cases, we take the lower end of the quoted range.

2. There is also the issue of simultaneity in the price function: see Wills (1978).

3. Two important studies estimating time series of computer price functions are Chow (1967) and Stoneman (1976).

4. For the other products, the problem was either that the price data were unreliable or non-existent, or that the product did not fit very easily into our classification.

5. This is only a very small subset of all the information published about each product: see Osborne and Kane (1981).

6. Characteristic (5) is simply the product of (3) and (4); the justification for including it is that the value of the instruction set is not just the number of instructions, but their content (Kilobits).

7. The interpretation of negative autocorrelation is unclear.

8. We do not test the null hypothesis of 'no effect', which we consider of limited interest.

9. Close inspection of Table 5.1 will show that the time series for the other coefficients show similar instability.

10 A detailed discussion of this is in Swann (1985d).

11. The price functions used in Chapter 7 are—and have to be—of much smaller dimension.

6 Quality Competition in Microprocessors

In Chapter 2 we argued that the value of quality innovation to the firm was the extent to which it could change the demand for the firm's product. We saw that there were two ways in which this happened, first by expanding market demand and second by improving the firm's competitive position. We saw, moreover, that the extent of any improvement in competitive position would depend on the nature of rivals' reactions. The purpose of this chapter is to describe the quality competition process in microprocessors, and the manner in which firms respond to the innovations of others. This chapter uses material from Swann (1985a).

Section 6.1 briefly shows how the various microprocessors are to be classified, and emphasizes the distinction between 'own design' products and 'second source' products. Section 6.2 describes the history of quality innovation in microprocessors in broad outline.

Section 6.3 attempts some formal analysis of the observed developments. In particular, we calculate simple probabilities which reveal the prevalence of clustering. These simple probabilities may be misleading to the extent that most quality innovations take place along the frontier of the product possibility set, and sometimes there are few empty spaces along this frontier. Nevertheless, weighted probabilities which take account of the available space on the frontier still suggest a strong tendency to cluster. We examine a simple hypothesis about possible influences on quality improvements.

Section 6.4 finds important differences in the behaviour of different firms. We suggest a simple technique for measuring the similarity of different firms' product strategies, and for describing firms as 'leaders' or 'followers'.

Section 6.5 examines the developments in this market from the perspective of spatial and product competition theory, and finds an important role for 'agglomeration' economies, or mutual economies accruing to firms producing similar designs. Section 6.6 summarizes the main conclusions.

6.1 Measuring the microprocessor

The first microprocessor was introduced in 1971, but because of the very rapid technical change that has taken place, the products that appeared at the end of 1981 give a quite different level of performance. Nevertheless, it is not perhaps too misleading to think of these recent designs as 'no more than' much higher quality versions of the earlier devices.

In Chapter 5, we made use of a dozen characteristics in our price functions. A glance at a comprehensive microprocessor data book—for example, Osborne and Kane (1981)—makes it clear that it was by no means an exhaustive set of characteristics. For the purposes of this chapter, however, there was a strong case for reducing the number of characteristics so that it is possible to describe the developments graphically.[1] In the end, the following classification (Table 6.1) has been adopted. It may be rather rough and ready, but it corresponds quite closely to classifications used in the trade press. It is reasonably

Table 6.1   Classification of Microprocessors

---

(1)   Bit size
4-, 8-, 12-, 16-, or 32-bit data bus;
there are also devices with an 8-bit external data bus and 16-bit internal data bus ($^8/_{16}$), and devices with a 16-bit external data bus and a 32-bit internal data bus ($^{16}/_{32}$).

(2)   Level of integration

CPU only:	processing logic alone
CPU + RAM:	processing logic plus read-and-write memory (RAM)
MC − ROM;	processing logic, RAM, and Input/Output circuitry
MC:	a single-chip microcomputer with processing logic, RAM, I/O, and program memory (ROM)
MC + A/D:	an extended single-chip microcomputer with analog to digital circuitry

(3)   Generation

A (first):	the simplest devices in the category
B (second):	improved devices
C (third):	the most advanced device within the category

Source: Swann (1985a)

satisfactory for describing developments up to the end of 1981, but it would not do for some of the more recent developments.[2]

The 'bit size' refers to the size of the data bus; this is an indication of the processing power of the device. The 'level of integration' describes the number of computer features incorporated into the one device. The term 'generation' is an essentially subjective[3] measure of the status of the device within its 'bit size'/'level of integration' category. Within any category there may be considerable difference between products. For example, within the '8/16-bit, processor logic only' category come four products: the Intel 8088, the Texas Instruments 9980, the Motorola 6809, and the Zilog Z800. While most technical writers would agree that these are similar products, they are certainly not identical, and not really minimally differentiated[4] (see Whitworth, 1980, and *Electronics*, 19 May 1981, p. 62). Nevertheless, the classification is probably the most useful three-way classification available, and as mentioned before it is widely used.[5]

Finally, it is important to make a distinction between 'own design' microprocessors and 'second source' products. Over the period, some twenty-two firms have produced and sold their own microprocessors, but these are not the only microprocessors that are sold. In microelectronics, there is a widespread practice of producing second-source products: these are (almost) identical copies of another manufacturer's design. The production of these copies may or may not be authorized by the original designer.

The production of second-source products is a rather special form of quality competition; some particularly important agglomeration economies operate here that do not apply to own-design products. For this reason, we discuss the development of own-design and second-source products separately.

6.2 Developments in microprocessors: an outline

Table 6.2 lists the main microprocessor producers who between them account for the greater part of the world market. Six firms have made at least five products of their own design, while a further sixteen have produced one or two designs of their own. Some of these firms have also produced a significant number of second-source products, while a further sixteen have produced one or more second-source products, but no designs of their own. Between 1971 and 1981, 203 separate products have been introduced, of which 69 are original designs, while 134 are

Table 6.2 Microprocessors produced by principal manufacturers, 1971–81

	Manufacturer	Own-design products	Second-source products
A	Intel	12	0
B	National Semiconductor	9	7
C	Texas Instruments	9	1
D	Motorola	7	5
E	Rockwell	5	2
F	Zilog	5	0
G	AMI	2	12
H	NEC	2	9
I	Fairchild	2	8
J	Mostek	2	3
K	Toshiba	2	1
L	General Instruments	2	0
M	Fujitsu	1	7
N	Hitachi	1	7
O	Signetics	1	7
P	Intersil	1	5
Q	Bell Labs	1	0
R	Data General	1	0
S	Electronic Arrays	1	0
T	Hewlett Packard	1	0
U	MOS	1	0
V	RCA	1	0
—	AMD	0	12
—	Siemens	0	8
—	Harris	0	7
—	Mitsubishi	0	7
—	SGS–ATES	0	6
—	ITT	0	4
—	AEG Telefunken	0	3
—	Matra–Harris	0	2
—	Philips	0	2
—	Plessey	0	2
—	Sharp	0	2
—	Marconi	0	1
—	Mitel	0	1
—	NCR	0	1
—	Sescosem	0	1
—	Thomson CSF	0	1
	Total	69	134

Source: Swann (1985a)

second-source products; in short, almost two-thirds are second-source products.[6]

The history of own-design product developments is described in Table 6.3. For each year the table presents the cumulative picture at the end of

Table 6.3 Product location history, 1971–81

1971–2

	CPU	CPU+RAM	MC−ROM	MC	MC+A/D
4A	A	.	.	.	.
4B	.	.	.	.	.
4C	.	.	.	.	.
8A	A	.	.	.	.
8B	.	.	.	.	.
8C	.	.	.	.	.
12A	.	.	.	.	.
8/16	.	.	.	.	.
16A	.	.	.	.	.
16B	.	.	.	.	.
16C	.	.	.	.	.
16/32	.	.	.	.	.
32A	.	.	.	.	.

1973

	CPU	CPU+RAM	MC−ROM	MC	MC+A/D
4A	a	.	.	C	.
4B	E	.	.	.	.
4C	.	.	.	.	.
8A	a	.	.	.	.
8B	A	.	.	.	.
8C	.	.	.	.	.
12A	K	.	.	.	.
8/16	.	.	.	.	.
16A	.	.	.	.	.
16B	.	.	.	.	.
16C	.	.	.	.	.
16/32	.	.	.	.	.
32A	.	.	.	.	.

1974

	CPU	CPU+RAM	MC−ROM	MC	MC+A/D
4A	a	.	.	c	.
4B	eA	.	.	.	.
4C	.	.	.	.	.
8A	a	.	.	.	.
8B	aDEOV	.	.	.	.
8C	.	.	.	.	.
12A	k	.	.	.	.
8/16	.	.	.	.	.
16A	BL	.	.	.	.
16B	.	.	.	.	.
16C	.	.	.	.	.
16/32	.	.	.	.	.
32A	.	.	.	.	.

1975

	CPU	CPU+RAM	MC−ROM	MC	MC+A/D
4A	a	.	.	c	.
4B	ea	.	.	E	.
4C	.	.	.	.	.
8A	a	.	.	.	.
8B	adeovBU	.	I	.	.
8C	.	.	.	.	.
12A	kP	.	.	.	.
8/16	.	.	.	.	.
16A	bl	.	.	.	.
16B	.	.	.	.	.
16C	.	.	.	.	.
16/32	.	.	.	.	.
32A	.	.	.	.	.

1976

	CPU	CPU+RAM	MC−ROM	MC	MC+A/D
4A	a	.	.	c	.
4B	ea	.	.	eB	.
4C	.	.	.	.	.
8A	a	.	.	.	.
8B	adeovbu	S	iA	AEL	.
8C	F	.	.	.	.
12A	kp	.	.	.	.
8/16	.	.	.	.	.
16A	bl	.	.	.	.
16B	C	.	.	.	.
16C	.	.	.	.	.
16/32	.	.	.	.	.
32A	.	.	.	.	.

1977

	CPU	CPU+RAM	MC−ROM	MC	MC+A/D
4A	a	.	.	c	.
4B	ea	.	.	ebGH	.
4C	.	.	.	.	.
8A	a	.	.	.	.
8B	adeovbu	sD	ia	aelJ	.
8C	fA	.	.	.	.
12A	kp	.	.	.	.
8/16	C	.	.	.	.
16A	bl	.	.	.	.
16B	cIR	.	.	.	.
16C	.	.	.	.	.
16/32	.	.	.	.	.
32A	.	.	.	.	.

1978				
	CPU	CPU+RAM	MC−ROM	MC	MC+A/D
4A	a	.	.	c	.
4B	ea	.	.	ebgh	.
4C	.	.	.	.	.
8A	a	.	.	.	.
8B	adeovbu	sd	ia	aeljA	A
8C	fa	.	.	J	.
12A	kp	.	.	.	.
8/16	cAC	.	.	.	.
16A	blB	.	.	.	.
16B	cir	.	.	C	.
16C	A	.	.	.	.
16/32	.	.	.	.	.
32A	.	.	.	.	.

1979				
	CPU	CPU+RAM	MC−ROM	MC	MC+A/D
4A	a	.	.	c	.
4B	ea	.	.	ebgh	.
4C	.	.	.	.	.
8A	a	.	.	.	.
8B	adeovbv	sd	ia	aeljaD	a
8C	fa	.	D	jDFH	.
12A	kp	.	.	.	.
8/16	cacD	.	.	.	.
16A	blb	.	.	.	.
16B	cir	.	.	.	.
16C	aF	.	.	.	.
16/32	.	.	.	.	.
32A	.	.	.	.	.

1980				
	CPU	CPU+RAM	MC−ROM	MC	MC+A/D
4A	a	.	.	c	.
4B	ea	.	.	ebgh	.
4C	.	.	.	.	.
8A	a	.	.	.	.
8B	adeovbu	sd	ia	aeljadB	a
8C	faB	.	dB	jdfhB	.
12A	kp	.	.	.	.
8/16	cacd	.	.	.	.
16A	blb	.	.	.	.
16B	cir	.	.	c	.
16C	afFK	.	.	.	.
16/32	D	.	.	.	.
32A	.	.	.	.	.

1981				
	CPU	CPU+RAM	MC−ROM	MC	MC+A/D
4A	a	.	.	c	.
4B	ea	.	.	ebgh	.
4C	.	.	.	.	CG
8A	a	.	.	.	.
8B	adeovbu	sd	ia	aeljadb	a
8C	fab	.	db	jdfhbCN	.
12A	kp	.	.	.	.
8/16	cacdF	.	.	.	.
16A	blb	.	.	.	.
16B	cir	.	C	c	.
16C	affkEM	C	.	.	.
16/32	dB	.	.	.	.
32A	AQT	.	.	.	.

Source: Swann (1985a)

the year, where all components introduced to that date are left in the sample.[7] The components are labelled A–V according to the manufacturer, as in Table 6.2; the capital letters represent new designs introduced during that year, while the lower-case letters represent products introduced before that year. The sources of data are as described at the start of Chapter 5.

The early developments (1971–74) were almost entirely in the 'CPU-only' category. The earliest microprocessors were 'first-generation' 4- and 8-bit designs, but 12-bit and some 16-bit designs appeared soon after. By the end of 1974, the most striking cluster is in the second-generation 8-bit, CPU–only category, where 5 of the 13 devices are located. The only product outside the CPU only category is the Texas Instruments TMS 1000, a 4-bit, single-chip microcomputer.

From 1975 to 1977, there are further additions to the 8-bit, CPU-only category, and a few further developments in the second-generation 16-bit category, but the most important development is the emergence of components with higher levels of integration than CPU-only. Of particular importance are the 4- and 8-bit, single-chip microcomputer categories.

In 1978 and 1979, many new designs are clustered in the 8-bit microcomputer category (second and third generation), but perhaps the most important development is the appearance of the third-generation 16-bit CPU, as well as the 8/16-bit category. One outlier, which still stands alone at the end of 1981, is a 16-bit, single-chip microcomputer (Texas Instruments TMS 9940).

Finally, in 1980 and 1981, the most interesting developments are in the third-generation 16-bit, CPU-only category, and the 16/32- and 32-bit categories.

Finally, mention must be made of the production of second-source microprocessors. Table 6.4 describes the most important second-source activity. Of the 134 second-source products introduced over the period, 115 are copies of products originally designed by five companies: Intel, Motorola, Texas Instruments, Zilog, and Mostek. The table shows which manufacturers have produced second-source versions of which products. The categories used are broader than those in Table 6.3: 'mp' refers to CPU-only and CPU + RAM, while 'mc' refers to MC − ROM, MC and MC + A/D.

Two points should be made. First, Intel's designs have attracted the greatest number of second sources: a total of 62 products are listed in the table. Motorola have also attracted a fair number of second sources (29 products). Zilog (11 products), Texas (7 products), and Mostek (6 products) are less important.

Secondly, within any product category, a second source is unlikely to copy the products of more than one original manufacturer. There are four exceptions to this—AMD, AMI, NEC, SGS–ATES—but there is a special reason in each case.[8] It is not unusual, however, to find a second source copying the 8-bit designs of one manufacturer and the 16-bit designs of another. For example, Signetics have copied the 8-bit designs of Intel (8080, 8048, etc.) and the 16-bit design of Motorola (68000).

6.3 Clustering in quality space

How much evidence of clustering is there? Inspection of Table 6.3 certainly suggests that products are not randomly scattered in product

Table 6.4 Second-source products

Second source	Intel				Motorola				Texas			Zilog			Mostek	Total
	8mp	8mc	8/16	16	8mp	8mc	8/16	16	8/16	16mp	16mc	8mp	8mc	16	8mc	
AMD	2	4	1	1	·	·	·	·	·	·	·	1	1	1	·	11
AMI	·	·	·	·	2	3	1	·	2	1	1	·	·	·	·	10
NEC	2	4	·	1	·	·	·	·	·	·	·	·	·	·	2	9
Fairchild	·	·	1	1	2	1	1	1	·	·	·	1	·	·	·	8
Mitsubishi	2	4	1	1	·	·	·	·	·	·	·	·	·	·	·	8
Siemens	2	4	1	1	·	·	·	·	·	·	·	·	·	·	·	8
Fujitsu	·	4	1	·	1	1	·	·	·	·	·	·	·	·	·	7
Hitachi	·	·	·	·	2	3	1	1	·	·	·	·	·	·	·	7
Harris	·	4	·	·	·	1	·	1	·	·	·	·	·	·	·	6
Signetics	1	4	·	·	·	·	·	·	·	·	·	1	·	·	·	6
National	1	4	·	·	·	·	·	·	·	·	·	·	·	·	·	5
SGS–ATES	·	·	1	1	·	·	·	·	1	·	1	·	1	·	·	5
Intersil	·	4	·	·	·	·	·	·	·	·	·	·	·	·	·	4
ITT	·	·	1	1	·	·	·	·	·	1	·	·	·	·	·	3
Matra–Harris	·	·	·	·	1	·	·	1	·	·	·	·	·	·	·	2
Mostek	·	·	·	·	1	·	·	1	·	·	·	·	·	·	·	2
Motorola	·	·	·	·	·	·	·	·	·	·	·	·	1	1	·	2
Philips	1	·	·	·	·	·	·	·	·	·	·	1	·	·	·	2
Sharp	·	·	·	·	1	·	·	·	·	·	·	1	·	·	·	2
Marconi	·	·	·	·	1	·	·	·	·	·	·	·	·	·	·	1
Mitel	·	·	·	·	1	·	·	·	·	·	·	·	·	·	·	1
NCR	·	·	·	·	·	·	·	·	·	·	·	·	·	·	1	1
Plessey	·	·	·	·	·	·	·	·	·	·	·	·	·	·	1	1
Sescosem	·	·	·	·	·	·	·	·	·	·	·	·	·	·	1	1
Texas	1	·	·	·	·	·	·	·	·	·	·	·	·	·	·	1
Thomson–CSF	·	·	·	·	·	·	·	·	·	·	·	·	·	1	·	1
Toshiba	·	·	·	·	·	·	·	·	·	·	·	·	·	·	1	1
Total	12	36	7	7	12	9	3	5	3	2	2	5	3	3	6	115

Source: Swann (1985a)

space. The cumulative picture at the end of 1981 can be described by a 'μ' shape: all but 3 of the 69 designs fall within the 'CPU-only' category, the 8-bit categories, and the 4-bit, single-chip microcomputer category (with or without analog to digital features).

The initial impression is that clustering is quite important, and we shall present some formal measures in a moment. It could be argued, however, that clustering is observed simply because the product locations that remain empty represent impossible, unsuitable, or unwanted products. Unfortunately, we do not have the evidence with which to endorse or refute this view. The sales data we have are for much broader categories than those used here. Moreover, we have no data on sales for the sparsely populated categories, and obviously there are no sales for the empty categories. Besides, there are undoubtedly problems of interpretation: sales data cannot express potential demand for non-existent products.

While there are obvious dangers in interpreting any non-uniformity in dispersion as 'clustering', our view on balance is that the observed pattern should be interpreted in this way. All the categories in Table 6.3 represent possible and suitable products in the sense that they could be made (given a sufficiently advanced technology) and sold. For example, there could undoubtedly be demand for products in between the 4-bit CPU and the 4-bit microcomputer, in the same way as there was demand for products in between the 8-bit CPU and the 8-bit, single-chip microcomputer. The emptiness of such locations is not simply a result of a lack of demand.

Some formal measures

At first sight it appears that an obvious way to test for clustering would be to test for uniformity of distribution in a contingency table. There are, however, considerable difficulties with such a test. Firstly, operational difficulties: to apply the chi-squared test for consistency with a hypothetical distribution, the rule of thumb is that the expected number of entries in any category should not be less than five. With 69 products, this would require a much smaller contingency table than we have drawn—at most 14 categories.

There are conceptual problems, too, with a test of this type. If we view the observed pattern as a sample from the history of microprocessors, we have difficulties with any assumption of random sampling: given rapid technical progress, the procedure which 'samples' particular products is not a random sampling procedure. If we try to get round this by treating the observed pattern as a sample from this year's population, we may run into a statistical dead end. If the observed pattern in any year represents the complete set of products in that year, then we are left with a question of interpretation, not a matter of inference from a small sample.

An alternative line of approach seems preferable. At any point, the innovating firm has three options: (a) to move 'horizontally' into an empty location in the existing product possibility set; (b) to extend the product possibility set in a 'vertical' direction—the terms 'horizontal' and 'vertical' are used in the sense defined by Abbott (1955); (c) to cluster. (We shall find it useful to subdivide options (a) and (c) later.) If we assume that the firm makes its innovation decision in any year on the basis of the pattern at the start of the year, then we can use the patterns in Table 6.3 to calculate probabilities.

In the context of the quality space defined by Table 6.3, we define clustering (option (c)) as the decision to locate in a category where there is already another product at the start of the year. If two firms move to the same (previously empty) location in the same year, we do not classify this as a move of type (c): it would be either (a) or (b).

We define 'horizontal' innovations (a) as qualities which do not extend the product possibility set. In Table 6.3, the product possibility set contains all product categories above and to the left—or north and west—of the existing products. Thus any horizontal innovation must be further west and no further south, or further north and no further east of an existing product.

Finally, we define 'vertical' innovations (b) as qualities which do extend the product possibility set. In Table 6.3, there will be no existing products that are further east and no further north, or further south and no further west than a vertical innovation.

Over the whole period, we calculate from Table 6.3 that of the 69 quality innovations, 8 count as horizontal innovations, 22 count as vertical innovations, and 39 count as clustering. Since the three options are—by our definition—mutually exclusive and exhaustive, we may model the quality innovation decision by a 'trinomial' distribution.[9] If we assume that the probabilities are constant over time and between firms—more on that later—then we construct the following 95 per cent confidence intervals for the probabilities of the three sorts of innovation:[10]

	lower limit	sample mean	upper limit
(a) horizontal	0.04	0.12	0.19
(b) vertical	0.21	0.32	0.43
(c) clustering	0.44	0.56	0.69

The fact that the confidence intervals do not overlap makes it quite clear that it will be easy to reject any hypotheses about the equality of probabilities: both the hypothesis of equal probabilities of vertical innovation and clustering, and the hypothesis of equal probabilities of horizontal innovation and vertical innovation are rejected at the 0.5 per cent level.[11]

From this perspective, clustering appears to be the prevalent quality innovation strategy. Moreover, if we take into account the very large number of second-source products that are produced (a special sort of clustering), the prevalence of clustering is even more pronounced. Taking these into account, the number of instances of clustering during the period rises to 173,[12] and the corresponding confidence intervals are:

	lower limit	sample mean	upper limit
(a) horizontal	0.01	0.04	0.07
(b) vertical	0.06	0.11	0.15
(c) clustering	0.80	0.85	0.90

It is hardly necessary to conduct tests of equality here!

'Space-adjusted' probabilities

There are, however, several possible objections to these simple measures. The possibility that different firms have different strategies is examined in Section 6.4. Another, and at first sight rather serious, objection is that in calculating these probabilities we are not taking account of the space available for different types of innovation. The preponderance of clustering may simply reflect the fact that there are few empty locations within the product possibility set, so that clustering is inevitable.

A glance at Table 6.3 might appear to dispel such anxieties, since there are so many empty spaces within the product possibility set. We must be careful, however, to look at the right measure of 'space'. We shall see below that practically all the clustering occurs in categories on the boundary of the product possibility set;[13] by the boundary we mean those locations in the product possibility set for which there is no other product in the set which lies further south and further east. Likewise, practically all the horizontal innovation occurs along the boundary.[14] The relevant measure of space, then, is more likely to be the number of empty locations along the boundary.

Table 6.5 extracts the relevant data from Table 6.3. For each year it breaks down the innovations into: horizontal interior, horizontal boundary, vertical, clustering interior and clustering boundary. The table also breaks down the existing product possibility set (at the start of the year) into: interior empty, boundary empty, interior occupied and boundary occupied. (We do not attempt to measure the space available for vertical innovations; in a sense it is very large, but it is difficult to say exactly how many locations outside the 'possibility' set become possible during a year.) In some years, 1977 for example, there are very few empty locations along the boundary; the high incidence of clustering on the boundary in that year may simply be the result of the limited number of empty locations on the boundary.

To examine this more formally, we calculate what may be termed 'space-adjusted' probabilities. The idea here is very simple. The ratio of the simple probabilities of horizontal innovation (a) to clustering (c) is given by their (simple) relative frequencies. Thus:

$$p_a/p_c = n_a/n_c$$

where the p is simple probability and the n is the number of innovations. The 'space-adjusted' probabilities simply adjust the numbers of innovations to reflect the space available for them—we take this to be the space on the boundary. Thus if L_e refers to the number of empty boundary locations and L_o to the number of occupied boundary locations, we define:

$$p_a^*/p_c^* = \frac{n_a/L_e}{n_c/L_o}$$

where the p^* is the 'space adjusted probability.

Since we cannot deal satisfactorily with space available for vertical innovation, we just compare the simple and space-adjusted conditional probabilities of horizontal innovation and clustering, given that the innovation is not a vertical innovation. For obvious reasons, these can only be compared when neither L is zero— that is from 1973 to 1981.

Table 6.5 Analysis of innovations and product possibility set

Year	Innovations					Product possibility set			
	Horizontal		Vertical	Clustering		Empty locations		Occupied locations	
	Interior	Boundary		Interior	Boundary	Interior	Boundary	Interior	Boundary
1971	0	0	1	0	0	—	—	—	—
1972	0	0	1	0	0	0	0	0	1
1973	0	1	3	0	0	0	2	0	2
1974	0	0	2	0	5	0	4	0	6
1975	0	0	2	0	3	0	5	0	7
1976	0	2	4	0	2	6	6	3	6
1977	0	1	0	0	7	9	3	3	10
1978	0	0	4	0	4	9	2	3	11
1979	1	0	0	1	5	19	9	12	6
1980	0	0	1	2	4	18	9	13	6
1981	0	3	4	1	5	18	9	13	7
Total	1	7	22	4	35				

The conditional probabilities of clustering are calculated from Table 6.5:

	1973	1974	1975	1976	1977	1978	1979	1980	1981
simple	0	1	1	0.5	0.88	1	0.86	1	0.66
adjusted	0	1	1	0.5	0.68	1	0.90	1	0.72

Apart from 1977, there is little difference between the two, and it suggests that the simple probabilities calculated above do not give a misleading impression of the relative probabilities of horizontal innovation and clustering.

A simple hypothesis about vertical innovation

The data in Table 6.5 suggest a simple but interesting hypothesis: the probability of vertical innovation may increase when the empty space on the boundary falls. Since this hypothesis is data-based, any test using these data would not be very demanding, and conventional significance criteria would be quite misleading. Nevertheless, it is interesting to examine the corresponding regression.

Using the data in Table 6.5, a regression of the (unconditional) probability of vertical innovation in each year against the number of empty locations on the boundary in that year for the period 1972–81 yields the following results (figures in parentheses are conventional parameter standard errors):

$$\frac{\text{vertical innovations}}{\text{all products introduced}} = \underset{(0.15)}{0.71} - \underset{(0.025)}{0.065}\ \text{empty locations}$$

$$R^2 = 0.80 \qquad DW = 1.93 \qquad SE = 0.25 \qquad df = 8$$

The interpretation of this is that as one previously empty location on the boundary of the product set becomes occupied this increases the probability of vertical innovation by 0.065. This would be an interesting hypothesis to examine with other products.

Rival reaction: the probability of following

We have seen the preponderance of clustering in this sample. It is interesting to look at this from a slightly different point of view. For any non-clustering innovation, what is the probability that it will be followed? How soon is it followed?

From Table 6.3 we see that there are 24 occupied locations by the end of 1981. Notice that this does not tally with the total number of non-clustering innovations in Table 6.5, since sometimes two or more firms move to the same empty location at the same time. Of the 24 occupied locations, 7 are occupied by one product only, but 2 of these 7 are only just introduced in 1981, and it is too early to say that they will not be followed. Basing our calculations on the remaining 22 products, we find that the probability of being followed is 17/22, or 77 per cent.

Of the 22 locations, 5 remain empty after three years (or more), 1 is followed after two years, 12 are followed after one year, and 4 are 'followed' in the same year. The implication is that any move tends to be followed quickly.

6.4 Strategies of individual firms

In this section we take a closer look at the product strategies of individual firms. Does a particular firm tend to move towards its rivals? Alternatively, does it tend to move away into less densely populated categories? Here we briefly discuss the strategies of the six main producers of own-designed microprocessors according to Table 6.2. These are Intel (A), National Semiconductor (B), Texas Instruments (C), Motorola (D), Rockwell (E), and Zilog (F). Table 6.6, derived in an obvious way from Table 6.3, describes the sequence of locations for these six companies.

First we shall compare these strategies in broad outline; then we shall make some formal comparisons. We see that different firms have different innovation probabilities. We also suggest a simple method for measuring the similarity of different firms' product strategies, and the extent to which a firm is a leader or a follower. This method makes use of ideas rather like the concepts of 'coherence' and 'phase difference' in spectral analysis.

A description of the strategies

Intel are the acknowledged market leader, not only in the sense of being first to locate in many of the categories that have subsequently become important clusters, but also in the sense of attracting the greatest number of second-source copies (see Section 6.2). Throughout the

Table 6.6 Product location sequence for six major microprocessor manufacturers

Intel (A)

	CPU	CPU+ RAM	MC– ROM	MC	MC+ A/D
4A	71	.	.	.	.
4B	74	.	.	.	.
4C	.	.	.	.	.
8A	71	.	.	.	.
8B	73	.	76	76,78	78
8C	77	.	.	.	.
12A	.	.	.	.	.
8/16	78	.	.	.	.
16A	.	.	.	.	.
16B	.	.	.	.	.
16C	78	.	.	.	.
16/32	.	.	.	.	.
32A	81	.	.	.	.

National Semiconductor (B)

	CPU	CPU+ RAM	MC– ROM	MC	MC+ A/D
4A	.	.	.	.	.
4B	.	.	.	76	.
4C	.	.	.	.	.
8A	.	.	.	.	.
8B	75	.	.	80	.
8C	80	.	80	80	.
12A	.	.	.	.	.
8/16	.	.	.	.	.
16A	74,78	.	.	.	.
16B	.	.	.	.	.
16C	.	.	.	.	.
16/32	81	.	.	.	.
32A	.	.	.	.	.

Texas Instruments (C)

	CPU	CPU+ RAM	MC– ROM	MC	MC+ A/D
4A	.	.	.	73	.
4B	.	.	.	.	.
4C	.	.	.	.	81
8A	.	.	.	.	.
8B	.	.	.	.	.
8C	.	.	.	81	.
12A	.	.	.	.	.
8/16	77,78	.	.	.	.
16A	.	.	.	.	.
16B	76	.	.	81	78
16C	.	81	.	.	.
16/32	.	.	.	.	.
32A	.	.	.	.	.

Motorola (D)

	CPU	CPU+ RAM	MC– ROM	MC	MC+ A/D
4A	.	.	.	.	.
4B	.	.	.	.	.
4C	.	.	.	.	.
8A	.	.	.	.	.
8B	74	77	.	79	.
8C	.	.	79	79	.
12A	.	.	.	.	.
8/16	79	.	.	.	.
16A	.	.	.	.	.
16B	.	.	.	.	.
16C	.	.	.	.	.
16/32	80	.	.	.	.
32A	.	.	.	.	.

Rockwell (E)

	CPU	CPU+ RAM	MC– ROM	MC	MC+ A/D
4A	.	.	.	.	.
4B	73	.	.	75	.
4C	.	.	.	.	.
8A	.	.	.	.	.
8B	74	.	.	76	.
8C	.	.	.	.	.
12A	.	.	.	.	.
8/16	.	.	.	.	.
16A	.	.	.	.	.
16B	.	.	.	.	.
16C	81	.	.	.	.
16/32	.	.	.	.	.
32A	.	.	.	.	.

Zilog (F)

	CPU	CPU+ RAM	MC– ROM	MC	MC+ A/D
4A	.	.	.	.	.
4B	.	.	.	.	.
4C	.	.	.	.	.
8A	.	.	.	.	.
8B	.	.	.	.	.
8C	76	.	.	79	.
12A	.	.	.	.	.
8/16	81	.	.	.	.
16A	.	.	.	.	.
16B	.	.	.	.	.
16C	79,80	.	.	.	.
16/32	.	.	.	.	.
32A	.	.	.	.	.

Source: Swann (1985a)

period, their strategy has been one of steadily improving the product, whether in terms of higher bit sizes, higher levels of integration, or a higher 'generation' product. Of all their products, perhaps the most important was the 8080 (8-bit, CPU-only, second-generation), introduced in 1973. It was the first product in arguably the most important cluster.

In terms of the crude categories used in this paper, Motorola, Zilog and Rockwell can be said to have followed Intel's lead, though they have certainly produced important innovations of their own. Motorola did not enter the 4-bit market with their own design,[15] but they have followed Intel into the other categories. Zilog, likewise, produced no 4-bit device, but have otherwise followed Intel, although their 8/16-bit product (Z800) was a little late, and represents—in a sense—a backward move. Rockwell have followed Intel, and also followed Texas Instruments into the 4-bit microcomputer category.

National Semiconductor's product profile fits into the 'μ' shape mentioned above, but the sequence they follow is a little unusual. They start with a 16-bit device, then introduce an 8-bit device, and follow that with a 4-bit microcomputer. A further 16-bit design is followed by more 8-bit products. In short, they have several times moved backwards. They have located in (mostly) the same categories as Intel, but the sequence has been sufficiently different that they cannot really be called a follower.

Texas Instruments' product strategy has been the most unusual. They started with a 4-bit microcomputer, and then decided to leapfrog the 8-bit category altogether and concentrate on the 16-bit category. Subsequently they introduced two 8/16-bit, CPU-only designs, but they never produced an 8-bit CPU of their own design. Following the trend of integration in 8-bit devices, they produced a 16-bit, single-chip microcomputer, a move that had not been followed by the end of 1981. Rather late in the day (1981), they introduced a third-generation, 8-bit microcomputer.

Like National Semiconductor, then, Texas Instruments appear to have moved into certain locations too soon, and have had to move backwards. Unlike National Semiconductor, and unlike the other main manufacturers, their product profile does not fit into the 'μ' shape. Moreover, it could not be said that they follow the product leader, Intel. Indeed, Texas Instruments' strategy seems to have been to locate as far away from Intel as possible. While Intel were producing 8-bit CPU designs, Texas were introducing a 4-bit microcomputer; while Intel were improving these 8-bit designs, Texas introduced a 16-bit microprocessor; while Intel were starting to produce third-generation, 16-bit, CPU-only designs, Texas introduced a second-generation, 16-bit, single-chip microcomputer; and finally, when Intel were announcing the first 32-bit CPU, Texas Instruments were improving their existing 16-bit CPU, and making a late entry into the third-generation, 8-bit microcomputer category.

Formal measures

As before, we can calculate simple probabilities of horizontal innovation, vertical innovation and clustering for the six main firms. The probabilities for the period 1971–81 are presented in Table 6.7. In view of the discussion above, it is not surprising to find that Intel and Texas Instruments have high probabilities of vertical innovation, while National Semiconductor and Motorola have high probabilities of clustering.

Table 6.7 Clustering, horizontal innovation, and vertical innovation probabilities for six firms

	Intel	National	Texas	Motorola	Rockwell	Zilog
Horizontal	0	0	0.22	0.14	0.20	0
Vertical	0.58	0.11	0.56	0.14	0.40	0.20
Clustering	0.42	0.89	0.22	0.72	0.40	0.80

We tested for significant differences between the probabilities for different firms by means of a conventional F-test for the equality of several means.[16] The hypothesis that different firms have the same probability of horizontal innovation gives an $F(5,26)$ statistic of 2.12, which is (just about) significant at the 10 per cent level; the hypothesis that different firms have the same probability of vertical innovation gives an $F(5,26)$ statistic of 4.42 which is significant at the 1 per cent level; finally, the hypothesis that different firms have the same probability of clustering gives an $F(5,26)$ statistic of 6.06, which is significant at the 0.5 per cent level. In short, there are important differences between firms.

We have also tried to construct a formal measure of the similarity between the strategies of different firms, and a measure by which to distinguish leaders and followers. A rather natural measure of similarity is the number of product locations that the two have in common. Likewise, a natural way to describe whether one firm leads or follows another is by the interval between one firm locating in a particular category and the other locating in that category. Loosely speaking, these measures are a little like the concepts of 'coherence' and 'phase difference' in spectral analysis. The coherence measure is a measure of correlation, while the phase difference is a measure of leading and lagging. Such devices are undoubtedly rather crude, but they could be useful in the analysis of competitive strategy.

Table 6.8 (a) and (b) shows the 'coherence' and 'phase difference' measures corresponding to Table 6.6. The 'coherence' measures are calculated from all the products introduced by these firms during

Table 6.8(a) 'Coherence' of product strategies for six firms, 1971–81

	Product locations in common					
	Intel	National	Texas	Motorola	Rockwell	Zilog
Intel	11					
National	3	8				
Texas	1	1	8			
Motorola	3	5	2	7		
Rockwell	4	3	0	2	5	
Zilog	2	2	2	2	1	4

Table 6.8(b) 'Phase difference' of product strategies for six firms, 1971–81*

	Follower					
	Intel	National	Texas	Motorola	Rockwell	Zilog
Leader						
Intel	=	+3	−1	+1.7	+0.75	+1
National	−3	=	+1	+0.2	−2	−2.5
Texas	+1	−1	=	0	†	+1
Motorola	−1.7	−0.2	0	=	+1.5	+1
Rockwell	−0.75	+2	†	+1.5	=	−2
Zilog	−1	+2.5	−1	−1	+2	=

*Mean difference between location dates in years
†no overlap

the period 1971–81. The elements on the principal diagonal show the number of locations occupied by each firm at some stage during the period. As expected, we find that the product strategy of Texas Instruments has little in common with that of any other producer. The other firms' product profiles have a considerable overlap with that of Intel.

The 'phase difference' measures show the mean difference between introduction dates for those product locations the two firms have in common. The table should be read as follows: if a particular element is positive, it implies that the leader (the relevant row) leads the follower (the relevant column) by the interval indicated; alternatively, if a particular element is negative, it implies that the column leads the row, so to speak. Thus, the entry +1.7 for (Intel, Motorola) implies that Intel leads Motorola by an average of 1.7 years.

As would be expected, Intel seems to lead all other manufacturers except Texas Instruments—the entry of −1 for (Intel, Texas) is based on a sample overlap of 1, and should not perhaps be taken too seriously.

6.5 Implications for product competition theory

In this section, we attempt to draw out the implications of the history of developments in microprocessors for the empirical value of product competition theory. It would be unrealistic to expect that the evidence presented here could decisively refute any of the theory outlined in Section 2.6. Nevertheless, it is hoped that the evidence will give some indication of the empirical usefulness of this theory for the analysis of product competition in high technology products such as microprocessors.

The view taken here is that in their current state of development, the various branches of spatial and product competition theory do not have a sufficiently fine structure to allow discrimination between competing branches on the strength of predictive ability alone. For example, we saw in Chapter 2 that various extensions to the Hotelling model no longer predicted clustering, but the pattern of non-clustering in each case cannot be predicted with precision. Any observed pattern of non-clustering could be consistent with several branches of the theory. For that reason, we shall give some attention to the realism of the assumptions on which the various branches of the theory are based.

Second-source production

First, let us examine the strategy of second-source production. This is a clear case of clustering, albeit a rather special one. Any model predicting the absence of clustering cannot therefore be fully appropriate for the analysis of all aspects of product competition in microprocessors. Is this an indication that the extensions discussed in Chapter 2 which predict dispersion are irrelevant here? We shall argue that they are by no means irrelevant, but rather that they are incomplete if they do not take account of agglomeration economies.

The demand for microprocessors is certainly not inelastic to product characteristics. Likewise, relocation costs are not negligible, although the costs involved in copying another device are much less than the costs involved in designing a new product. Even so, it is interesting to observe that second sources rarely copy the products of more than one manufacturer in a particular category.[17] Consumers are usually unable to find any important differences between the second-source product and the original product. There is no brand loyalty to the second source, and so the sales of the second-source product may be volatile.[18]

The nature of conjectural variations is a little uncertain, essentially because microprocessor manufacturers have a somewhat ambivalent attitude to those who produce second-source copies of their products. Some manufacturers have strongly discouraged any second-source production, resorting to law suits if necessary. Others actively encourage a small number of authorized second sources, and tolerate some unauthorized second sources (Osborne and Kane, 1981, Chapter on the 8080; Wilson *et al.*, 1980, Chapter 4; *Electronics*, 15 May 1975, p. 74, and 15 March 1979, p. 56). The reason is that while the second-source product will inevitably compete with the original product, and often at a lower price,[19] the existence of a second source has been seen to convey some benefits on the original producer. These arise for two reasons. Firstly, several microprocessor manufacturers have on occasion had severe production problems, and buyers have faced supply shortages. Against this background, those buying large quantities of a particular microprocessor see the existence of an alternative source as an insurance policy. Secondly, the microprocessor will rarely be used alone: it is almost invariably used in conjunction with support devices, development aids, software. To the extent that a second source increases the total sales of a microprocessor, it will also increase total sales of these other items.

The importance of agglomeration economies for the second source is quite evident. Firstly, the manufacturer can economize on the otherwise substantial design and development costs. Secondly, he has much lower technical uncertainty as the original producer has already shown that the product is technically feasible. Thirdly, part of his market uncertainty is reduced as the success of the original product demonstrates the strong demand for the product. For these two reasons, second-source production is seen to be relatively free of risks. Finally, there are the substantial externalities that accrue from producing a standard product: for example, the existence of support devices, development systems and software produced by the original manufacturer, or indeed another second source.

Own designs

Next we consider the implications of the observed pattern of product competition in own-design microprocessors. While there was some doubt about whether the observed pattern represented clustering, we saw that many firms had a strong tendency to follow the leader. Not only did they locate in the same categories as the leader, but their products were introduced in the same sequence as the leader's. It seems fairly reasonable to interpret this as a tendency to cluster. Nevertheless, this tendency was not observed for all firms. For one firm, National Semiconductor, the locations were more or less the same as the leader, but the sequence was not, while for another, Texas Instruments, neither the locations nor the sequence coincide.

The observed clustering has the same implications as before for the theory discussed in Section 2.6. Once again, we would not argue that this makes the extensions which predict dispersion irrelevant, but rather that there are sufficient agglomeration economies to ensure clustering. The demand is clearly not inelastic, and relocation costs are much higher for the design of a new product than for the copying of a new product.[20] There is an element of brand loyalty here, so that even if the products of two manufacturers are similar, the repeat buyer will not switch from one product to another in a random fashion. For this reason, the argument that clustering promotes sales uncertainty is somewhat less relevant. On the other hand, the prospect of rival reaction seems more likely. The incidental benefits that arise from having a second source do not apply when the producer has a close rival producing a similar but differentiated product.

Agglomeration economies remain important, although some of the special economies that applied to the second-source product do not apply here. The agglomeration economies are essentially of two types: 'infrastructure' and informational externalities. There are 'infrastructure' advantages to producing a conventional product because, for example, some general-purpose support devices can be used by any microprocessor conforming to certain design conventions, and memory components are widely available for a 4-, 8- or 16-bit bus, but not so easily for unconventional sizes. In a few cases, firms have designed their products so that they can run software originally intended for other devices, a considerable 'infrastructure' economy.[21] Barron and Curnow (1979, Chapter 5) discuss other examples.

The informational externalities were mentioned before in the context of second-source production, and they are also important here. The greater initial success of the 8-bit microprocessors (especially the 8080 and 6800) than the 16-bit designs led some entrant firms to revise their estimates of the relative sizes of the 8-bit and 16-bit markets. Moreover, some would argue (for example, Barron and Curnow, 1979, pp. 69–70) that the true importance of the microprocessor as an innovation was not simply producing a miniature computer—which was by no means a new idea—but rather in demonstrating that small computers could be used for all sorts of applications never before thought of. In this sense, the success of the early products conveyed an informational externality to prospective entrants.

For a product subject to such rapid technical change, moreover, there are informational externalities about the technical feasibility of production. Perhaps the most important is what engineers in the industry call 'coming down the learning curve together'. Those who make the same product as other producers are in a position to exchange technical information. It might be thought that such information would be a jealously guarded secret, and in principle it might be. In practice, however, there has been a high degree of cross-fertilization, chiefly as a result of the close geographical location of many of the main American manufacturers and the high staff mobility. It is evident from some of the law suits that have attempted to stop such cross-fertilization that it is information from firms making similar products which is especially valuable (see *Electronics*, 13 November 1975, p. 38, and 25 December 1975, p. 37). Given that cross-fertilization is a fact of life in the industry, it is least risky for the manufacturer to locate in a position (both geographically and in product space) where he can benefit.[22]

Conclusion

The predominant tendency for firms to cluster can then be explained in at least two ways:

1 Firms are risk-averse and find the risks of clustering less serious than the risks of isolation.
2 they are not particularly risk-averse and are encouraged to cluster by the forces at work in the unmodified Hotelling model.

In view of the arguments above, we incline towards the first explanation.

What, though, of the two firms who have not shown this tendency to cluster? A variety of explanations might be offered, for example:

1 They are risk-averse but they perceive the risks of clustering to be greater than the risks of isolation (so they conform to some of the extensions to the Hotelling model mentioned in Section 1).
2 They are not particularly risk-averse, and although they agree that the risks of isolation may exceed the risks of clustering, they realize that demand is elastic with regard to characteristics, and find the potential rewards to radical innovation decisive.

The first explanation undoubtedly has its virtues. The two firms, National Semiconductor and Texas Instruments, are very large and produce a very wide range of semiconductor products of their own design. Isolation is not so risky for such firms, as they can to some extent provide their own infrastructure. Moreover, it is possible that such firms would be more likely to encounter rival reaction if they locate in a cluster.

Nevertheless, we incline to the second interpretation, though the two need not be mutually exclusive. Both these firms, but especially Texas Instruments, have a reputation for competitive or even aggressive pricing (see Sciberras, 1977, Chapter 5). A risk-averse firm would surely prefer to avoid such intense price competition. Moreover, Texas Instruments have produced only one second-source product; as we saw, the second-source strategy is particularly suitable for the risk-averse firm. And finally, if only for reasons of naïve diversification, the large firm is able to be less averse to risk.

Notes

1. Multidimensional cluster analysis could be used, but it is far from clear what would be the appropriate relative weights for discrepancies in different directions.
2. Such as, for example, the i**APX** series from Intel, where the degree of integration is not just a matter of processing logic, memory, input/output circuitry and analog/digital circuitry, but more importantly, the operating system and high-level languages—see *Microprocessors and Microsystems*, September 1980, pp. 291–2.
3. I am grateful to Richard Kaczynski for helpful discussions on the relative merits of various microprocessors.
4. Such a classification may, therefore, bias the results towards clustering.
5. Another method of measuring the microprocessor is the benchmark test: that is, measuring the performance at running various benchmark programs. Penney (1977) calculated five benchmark measurements for various microprocessors. It appears that the ranking of devices depends on the program chosen, which suggests that while such measurements are interesting, they are less useful for our purposes.
6. The precise number depends on the definition adopted: here, extensive families of similar designs have been reduced to a few key members.
7. It has often been difficult to establish the dates at which manufacturers stop active marketing of an old design, and even then the product will still be sold to serve replacement demand.
8. The Intel and Zilog 8-bit 'mp' products are sufficiently similar that NEC would find that the joint fixed costs were little more than the fixed costs for any individual product. AMI appear to copy the 8/16-bit designs of two manufacturers, but the Motorola 6809 is really part of Motorola's 8-bit range, while the Texas Instruments 9980 is really part of Texas's 16-bit range. Manufacturers have cultivated AMD and SGS–ATES as second sources, the former because they have a reputation for reliability and quality in production, and the latter because they are one of the few European manufacturers.
9. That is, a multinomial distribution with three exhaustive and mutually exclusive categories.
10. Assuming var$(\hat{p}_i) = \hat{p}_i(1-\hat{p}_i)/n$.

11. This is a simple test of the equality of two means, using the multinomial variance estimator in Note 10, and a normal approximation to the multinomial. The covariance of any two probability estimators is zero.
12. The number of innovations does not, of course, change.
13. The exceptions to the rule would certainly not be 'interior' innovations in a larger characteristics space.
14. The observation in Note 13 applies here, too.
15. They did produce a copy of the Texas Instruments TMS 1000.
16. See, for example, Mood *et al.* (1974), pp. 435ff; we assume a normal approximation to use this test.
17. Notwithstanding the exceptions in Note 8, this could be because copying costs are not trivial. Alternatively, it could be for reasons of competitive strategy.
18. Actually, second-source products may have minor differences from the original, but these rarely qualify as product differentiation.
19. They can afford to set lower prices as they do not have to recoup such large development costs as the original designer.
20. There is an additional relocation cost: firms who discontinue a line will lose the goodwill of existing users who require replacements.
21. The Zilog Z80, the Intel 8085, and the National Semiconductor NSC 800 all have instruction sets that are (different) supersets of the Intel 8080 instruction set.
22. This might be by formal technology exchange pact or by more informal trade. See Webbink (1977, Chapter 4B) and Braun and MacDonald (1978, Chapter 9, especially pp. 129ff).

7 An Exploratory Econometric Analysis of Quality Choice: The Microprocessor

The analysis of quality and quantity choice in Chapter 2 provided differential demand equations which could be estimated given a time series of price functions and a corresponding time series of quality and quantity choices. We saw that even if we only have data on aggregate sales of individual qualities, it is still possible to estimate a quality choice function. This chapter attempts such an econometric analysis.

We call it an 'exploratory' analysis because the available data are not ideal: firstly, the time series is (inevitably for such a new product) rather short; secondly, there are frequent redefinitions of product categories (again, a common feature of data on new products). Nevertheless, we present the results as an illustration of what could prove to be a powerful technique with more sympathetic data.

Section 7.1 describes the broad trends in the use of different types of semiconductors. Sales of integrated circuits have come to dominate sales of all other semiconductors, but sales of the more advanced integrated circuits are still a fairly small proportion of total integrated circuit sales.

Section 7.2 discusses some preliminaries to estimation; in particular: the question of how we should carry out a demand analysis with data on aggregate sales of different quality categories; the appropriate form of demand equation; and a method of estimation with 'non-observations'. Section 7.3 presents the regression results.

7.1 The growth in demand for microelectronic components

In terms of the dichotomy of Section 2.5, a successful quality innovation may improve a firm's competitive position, or it may increase market demand (or both). The improvement in competitive position comes about when existing consumers switch from an existing quality to the new quality; the increase in market demand happens when a new consumer buys the new quality, having previously been unwilling to buy any of the existing qualities. Either way, we would expect the successful quality innovation to be accompanied by a relatively high growth rate of sales for the new quality—relative to the growth of sales for other qualities, that is.

Given the preponderance of vertical quality innovation, the interesting question is whether the growth in use of microelectronic components has been concentrated in the high quality categories, or whether it has been evenly spread across all categories. If the former, it suggests that vertical quality innovation has been a successful strategy; if the latter, it suggests that the vertical quality innovation has been less successful.

Starting at a very aggregated level, we find that the share of integrated circuit sales in total American sales of semiconductors (diodes, transistors, integrated circuits, and other semiconductors) rose from 1 per cent to 75 per cent over the period 1961–80 (Electronic Industries Association: *Electronic Market Data Book*, various years). Integrated circuits represent (broadly speaking) the high quality category here, so there could hardly be any doubt about the success of the integrated circuit as a quality innovation.

For more disaggregated categories, the picture is essentially the same. As a proportion of American consumption (domestic sales by American manufacturers plus imports) of all categories of integrated circuit, the share of the simplest integrated circuits (Standard Logic) fell over the period 1971–82 from 92 per cent to below 25 per cent, although it was still (in 1982) one of the two largest categories (*Electronics Annual Surveys*, various years). The shares of RAM (random access memory) and ROM (read-only memory)—devices of intermediate sophistication—each rose over the same period by a factor of five (from about 4 per cent each to over 20 per cent each). The shares of microprocessors and microcomputers, perhaps the most sophisticated of the categories, have risen over the same period from nothing to 5 and 10 per cent respectively. These last two categories have shown the fastest percentage rate of growth, but still represent two of the smallest categories at this level of disaggregation.

At the finest degree of disaggregation available for 1981—there are problems of comparability which make a time series difficult to construct[1]—it becomes evident that within each of the above categories, the highest quality components account for a fairly small proportion of the sales of that category. Thus, sales of Advanced Schottky TTL are only about 1 per cent of total American 'Standard Logic' sales (*Electronics*, 13 January 1983). Likewise, sales of the bipolar CPU account for only 7 per cent of CPU sales, the 16-bit microcomputer about 1 per cent of single-chip microcomputer sales, fast static RAM about 10 per cent of RAM sales, and EEPROM about 4 per cent of ROM sales (*Electronics*, 13 January 1983). Nevertheless, this need not imply low growth rates.

What does this tell us? Rapid quality innovation need not be the cause of a high rate of growth of market demand for microelectronic components; the high growth rate may simply be a result of rapid 'pure' diffusion. Nevertheless, from the innovators point of view, rapid quality innovation has been successful if it promotes a relatively rapid rate of growth for the new quality, irrespective of whether it does this by increasing market demand or improving the firm's competitive position. From this perspective, the quality innovation observed in microelectronics appears to have been rather successful.

7.2 Some preliminaries to estimation

In Section 2.3 we argued that the analysis of quality and quantity choice using aggregate data must take account of 'pure' diffusion, but we saw that it is difficult to say how exactly that should be modelled.[2] The argument was, however, that equations in value shares might be less sensitive to specification bias from ignoring pure diffusion. We shall see in the next section that it is quite hard enough to model quality choice without having to worry about 'pure' diffusion. This alone would be reason enough to use demand equations in value shares; but in addition, equations in value shares are particularly suitable for a 'complete system' analysis of demand (as demonstrated by Deaton and Muellbauer, 1980).

Aggregate sales of different quality categories

The analysis of Chapter 2 provided differential demand equations, and we saw that these could—under some assumptions—be applied to aggregate data on sales of different quality categories. Suppose that the sales data classifies the different qualities by means of k characteristics, and that for characteristic i the data recognizes n_i different grades. The total number of categories in the contingency table is given by:

$$N = \prod_{i=1}^{k} n_i$$

The conventional complete system approach would express demand for a particular category as a function of the prices of all N categories. In quality demand analysis, the special dependence of demand on local adjustments to the price function means that the demand for any category is a function of its own price and the price derivatives in the directions of each of the k characteristics. In this way, quality demand analysis could be a very useful means of economizing on parameters. For small differences between different categories, there need only be one derivative per characteristic. For larger differences, it may be a good idea to introduce two derivatives per characteristic, one for a greater amount of the characteristic and one for a lesser amount; ideally these would be equal (and opposite), but they need not be.

The appropriate parameterization

Any differential demand equation would be approximated by an equation in first differences for estimation with time series data. In this context, we are so short of degrees of freedom anyway that it would be desirable to turn the equation in first differences into an equation in levels. This can be done at the risk of introducing positive first order autocorrelation.[3]

Following equations 2.5 and 2.6 and the subsequent argument in Section 2.2, a natural value share demand equation is:

$$w(z_i) = a_i + b_i \frac{x}{\pi} + c_i p(z_i) + d_i' p'(z_i) + u_i \tag{7.1}$$

where $w(z_i)$ is the share of quality category z_i in total expenditure, x/π is real expenditure, $p(z_i)$ is the price function evaluated at the particular quality category, and the vector $p'(z_i)$ represents the derivatives of the price function in the directions of the k different characteristics. An alternative form would be linear in the logs of real expenditure and prices (as in the 'Almost Ideal Demand System' of Deaton and Muell-bauer, 1980). In this particular application, however, there would be difficulties in using the logs of prices, as we shall see below.

Estimation with non-observations

The problem with this equation is that during the sample period, the number of quality categories changes as new qualities appear and old qualities disappear. Thus some of the derivatives in (7.1) are undefined in various periods but not in others. We could avoid this problem by restricting our sample to periods where the set of available qualities is constant, but that is no use when we are very short of degrees of freedom.

The question is, therefore, what value should we give to the undefined derivatives? In a sense, the prices of non-existent adjacent quality categories are infinite, and we could indeed attach very high values to those undefined prices. Nevertheless, we are reluctant to do this, because the introduction of a very large value for the derivative would lead to an arbitrarily large partial variance for that regressor. In turn this would lead to arbitrarily small coefficient standard errors and grossly distorted significance tests.

For this reason we adopt an alternative parameterization. The natural approach in such circumstances is to make the undefined entity a denominator, so that in 'ill-defined' cases, the value of the regressor becomes zero—this would not lead to arbitrarily large partial variances. Following this reasoning, we adopt the following parameterization:

$$w(z_i) = a_i + b_i \frac{x}{\pi} + c_i p(z_i) + \sum_{j=1}^{k} d_{ij} \frac{p(z_i)}{p(z_j)} + u_i \qquad (7.2)$$

Here the cross-price effects involve the price ratios with respect to the adjacent quality categories, $\{z_j : j=1, \ldots, k\}$. If a particular quality category, z_j ($i \neq j$), is empty in some periods, then the price ratio can naturally be put equal to zero. (If the category z_i is empty in some period, then we would obviously omit that period from the sample.) The zero price ratio will not distort the partial variance, but if we tried to re-parameterize (7.2) to put the prices in logs, the zero price ratio would go to minus infinity.

7.3 Quality choice: different qualities of microprocessor

As we said before, this is an 'exploratory' analysis because the available data are by no means ideal. First, inevitably for a new product, the time series is rather short; the first microprocessor was introduced in 1971, and the *Electronics Annual Survey* estimates of microprocessor sales do not disaggregate these sales before 1974.[4] Second, the available data are much more aggregated than we would ideally like. The *Electronics Annual Market Surveys* use a classification which distinguishes eight types of microprocessor and microcomputer, using two characteristics: bit size (4, 8, 16, 32) and degree of integration (microprocessor, microcomputer). Contrast this with the 65-category classification used in Chapter 6.[5] Moreover, it is not clear that the products in the microcomputer categories are necessarily higher quality products than those in the corresponding microprocessor category; they are of higher quality in one respect but may be inferior in others.

Third, again a common feature of data on new products, the best source we have makes frequent redefinitions of the product categories. Clearly, aggregate product categories must change to reflect the product life cycle, but 'non-nested'[6] redefinitions cause great difficulties in historical (let alone econometric) work. Finally, and related to this, it is our impression that the data are not very reliable, and they are clearly subject to large revisions.

The results

Table 7.1 shows the estimates for equation 7.2, using *Electronics Survey* data, 1974–83. Only four equations were estimated; there were not enough observations on the other categories to allow estimation.[7] The 4-bit microprocessor equation has two price ratio variables, corresponding to the two adjacent categories: the 8-bit microprocessor and the 4-bit microcomputer. The same applies to the 4-bit microcomputer equation. For the reasons discussed in the last section, the other two equations have three price ratio terms. The 8-bit microprocessor has three adjacent categories: the 4- and 16-bit microprocessors, and the 8-bit microcomputer. The same applies to the 16-bit microprocessor. The price data come from the same source as those in Chapter 5.[8]

For two of the equations, the equation standard errors are remarkably small, and in view of the very small number of degrees of freedom, the parameter standard errors are not unduly high. Indeed, some of the

Table 7.1 System of regression estimates for quality choice

Dependent variable: share of total expenditure

4-bit microprocessor

	Constant	Real Exp.	P_{4mp}	P_{4mp}/P_{8mp}	P_{4mp}/P_{4mc}
coeff.	−0.24	−0.053	0.036	0.073	0.17
SE	(0.053)	(0.041)	(0.0029)	(0.12)	(0.038)
CLME	0.48	0.62	8.6	0.21	0.66

$R^2=0.99$ ESE$=0.031$ DW$=1.77$ $N=10$

8-bit microprocessor

	Contant	Real Exp.	P_{8mp}	P_{8mp}/P_{4mp}	P_{8mp}/P_{16mp}	P_{8mp}/P_{8mc}
coeff.	0.098	−0.11	−0.0072	0.20	0.054	0.059
SE	(0.033)	(0.099)	(0.0054)	(0.14)	(1.8)	(0.20)
CLME	0.35	1.17	21.6	0.82	0.065	0.59

$R^2=0.68$ ESE$=0.13$ DW$=1.03$ $N=10$

16-bit microprocessor

	Constant	Real Exp.	P_{16mp}	P_{16mp}/P_{8mp}	P_{16mp}/P_{32mc}	P_{16mp}/P_{16mc}
coeff.	0.162	−0.296	−0.00019	−0.0129	7.49	−0.0812
SE	(0.0037)	(0.108)	(0.000045)	(0.0085)	(2.17)	(0.0368)
CLME	0.34	0.12	227.	1.47	0.0058	0.341

$R^2=0.96$ ESE$=0.014$ DW$=2.39$ $N=10$

4-bit microcomputer

	Constant	Real Exp.	P_{4mc}	P_{4mc}/P_{8mc}	P_{4mc}/P_{4mp}
coeff.	0.146	0.120	−0.0092	0.45	0.025
SE	(0.26)	(0.12)	(0.025)	(0.75)	(0.33)
CLME	0.344	0.739	3.66	0.121	0.276

$R^2=0.81$ ESE$=0.11$ DW$=1.15$ $N=10$

parameter standard errors are incredibly low. For example, the conventionally quoted t-statistic corresponding to the coefficient on own price in the 4-bit microprocessor equation is over 12! This reflects a surprisingly high partial variance for the own price variable, which is partly due to the parameterization chosen.[9]

Two of the Durbin–Watson statistics are disturbingly low (though the sample is too small for a precise critical value). This suggests that we would need to pay attention to the dynamic specification—hardly surprising for a new good. The table also shows the critical levels of measurement error for each regressor, as described in Chapter 5. These are generally quite high for the own price—hence the large partial variances—but they are sometimes alarmingly low for the price ratio terms. For example, the coefficient on P_{8mp}/P_{16mp} in the 8-bit micropro-cessor equation is 0.065; this means that if random measurement errors could perturb that price ratio from, say, one quarter to one third, then measurement error bias could be very serious.

Interpretation

Equations in value shares are easily misinterpreted. The most important point to remember is that the coefficients of a value share equation need not have the same sign as the conventional elasticity; indeed, the two will commonly have opposite signs. There are, however, simple relation-ships between these coefficients and the elasticities.

From Shephard's lemma we know that the partial derivative of total expenditure with respect to the price of good i (holding real income constant) gives the demand for good i: $\partial x/\partial p_i = q_i$. It is then trivial to show that $\partial \ln x/\partial \ln p_i = w_i$, where $w_i = p_i q_i/x$. We can use this result in an obvious manner to show that:

$$\frac{\partial \ln w_i}{\partial \ln p_i} = 1 + \frac{\partial \ln q_i}{\partial \ln p_i} - w_i$$

$$\frac{\partial \ln w_i}{\partial \ln(p_i/p_j)} = -\frac{\partial \ln w_i}{\partial \ln p_j} = -\frac{\partial \ln q_i}{\partial \ln p_j} + w_j$$

$$\frac{\partial \ln w_i}{\partial \ln x/\pi} = \frac{\partial \ln q_i}{\partial \ln x/\pi} - 1 \qquad (7.3)$$

The parameters of the value share equation represent partial deriva-tives, and (7.3) can easily be rearranged to give the following relation-ships between elasticities and the equation parameters:

$$\frac{\partial \ln q_i}{\partial \ln p_i} = \frac{p_i}{w_i} \frac{\partial w_i}{\partial p_i} + w_i - 1$$

$$\frac{\partial \ln q_i}{\partial \ln p_j} = \frac{-(p_i/p_j)}{w_i} \frac{\partial w_i}{\partial (p_i/p_j)} + w_j$$

$$\frac{\partial \ln q_i}{\partial \ln x/\pi} = \frac{(x/\pi)}{w_i} \frac{\partial w_i}{\partial (x/\pi)} + 1 \qquad (7.4)$$

Table 7.2   Price and expenditure elasticities evaluated at mean sample values

Consumption of 4-bit microprocessors	
Elasticity	
Price (4 mp)	+1.1
Price (8mp)	+0.011
Price (4mc)	+0.020
Real expenditure	+0.88
Consumption of 8-bit microprocessors	
Elasticity	
Price (8mp)	−1.4
Price (4mp)	−1.2
Price (16mp)	+0.053
Price (8mc)	−0.012
Real expenditure	+0.85
Consumption of 16-bit microprocessors	
Elasticity	
Price (16mp)	−1.1
Price (8mp)	+0.88
Price (32mp)	−0.81
Price (16mc)	+0.53
Real expenditure	−0.25
Consumption of 4-bit microcomputers	
Elasticity	
Price (4mc)	−0.98
Price (8mc)	−0.46
Price (4mp)	+0.13
Real expenditure	+1.2

Table 7.2 evaluates these elasticities at the sample mean values for prices, price ratios, real expenditure and value shares. With the exception of the 4-bit microprocessor equation, the own-price elasticities are sensible enough. Since adjacent quality categories are clearly substitutes, we would expect positive cross-price elasticities, but of the ten point estimates, four are negative. We would expect the highest quality categories—presumably the 16-bit microprocessor—to have the largest total expenditure elasticity, but ironically the 16-bit microprocessor has a negative elasticity.

One final point of interpretation. What would the estimated coeffi-cients imply about the effectiveness of quality innovation? We saw in Section 2.5 that the quality innovation can be described as a 'bulge' in the price function. If the quality innovation is to concentrate sales at a particular quality, aggregate demand at that quality should have a large own-price elasticity. This would in turn require moderate to large cross-price elasticities at adjacent qualities. If the quality innovation is to generate extra market demand, aggregate demand at that quality should have a large real expenditure elasticity.

Notes

1. This is a problem with the *Electronics Annual Surveys*, but it is still the most detailed source.
2. The exact shape of the pure diffusion curve is uncertain.
3. Much of the literature on complete systems of demand equations has paid relatively little attention to dynamic specification.
4. The two most important categories in the earlier years were the 4-bit microprocessor and the 8-bit microprocessor.
5. Ideally we would like data disaggregated by product and by buyer. The former is notoriously difficult to obtain, and many manufac-turers treat brand sales as proprietary information. Some market research surveys have collected data on purchases by individual buyers, but there is practically no time series dimension to these data, and moreover such data are very expensive.
6. We use the term in the statistical sense: non-nested revisions involve new categories which have an ill-defined intersection with earlier categories.
7. There were only 2 degrees of freedom for the 8-bit microcomputer category.
8. The category 'prices' represent the average prices of what are thought to be the most important products in the category, but in the absence of detailed market shares, these averages are likely to be subject to some error.
9. The high partial variance is almost entirely a result of the earliest observation (a very high price). If the parameterization used the logs of prices, that observation would make a much smaller contribution to the partial variation.

8 Three Case Studies of the Application of Microelectronics

As we have argued throughout this study, it is important both for the theory of innovation and for the theory of demand to understand how the demand for microelectronics has been influenced by rapid quality innovation. The econometric demand analysis of the last chapter was one way of looking at this question; in this chapter we take a rather different approach.

We present three case studies of the use of microelectronics which try to assess the importance of component quality for that application. As we saw in the discussion of computer system measurement in Chapter 3, it is possible to estimate what the application requires of the technology. Then using the data on developments in the technology (especially Chapter 4, but also Chapters 5 and 6), we can assess to what extent the use of microelectronics in the application has been held back by insufficient quality of the components. It is very unlikely that component quality is the only constraint on the development of the application; for that reason we shall mention some of the other important economic influences.

The three case studies are presented in Sections 8.1–8.3: microprocessor control of car engines, microelectronic telephone exchanges, and electronic calculators. Each case study is in five parts. The first part describes the possible uses of microelectronics. The second part discusses whether the successful use of microelectronics in this application depends on the availability of high quality components. The third part discusses some of the other economic issues that have influenced the use of microelectronics. The fourth part gives a brief history of the use of microelectronics in the area. Finally, the fifth part summarizes the case study and tries to answer the question: to what extent has quality innovation in microelectronic components led to increased demand for microelectronics in this application?

The reader unfamiliar with the technology may find the case studies heavy going. For this reason, the main conclusions are summarized together in Section 8.4, where we draw out their implications for the theory of demand. Section 8.4 also summarizes some of the main findings of other case studies in the literature.

8.1 Microprocessor control of car engines

Applications

(a) Engine control
The most important application of microelectronics in cars is probably engine control. A variety of engine control techniques are used to improve fuel economy and reduce exhaust pollution. The most important of these techniques are ignition tuning control (or spark control), closed-loop control of the air to fuel ratio (sometimes called the closed-loop carburettor), exhaust gas recirculation (EGR), and electronic fuel injection (EFI). The details of these techniques are described in *Electronics*, 20 November 1980.

To some extent, fuel economy and restriction of exhaust pollution are conflicting objectives. The air to fuel mixture which minimizes pollution—the 'stoichometric' region—is not the same as that which maximizes fuel economy. Even so, a compromise is attainable which satisfies the American emission regulations (see below) and still gives fuel consumption figures some 10 per cent better than can be achieved with conventionally controlled engines (Aono and Hata, 1981).

An illustrative numerical example will show the possible private value of this fuel economy. For a car meeting the 1980 American regulation figure of 20 miles per gallon and travelling 15,000 miles per annum, a 10 per cent improvement in fuel economy represents a saving of about 70 gallons or $200 per annum. The capitalized value of this saving might be $400.[1] This is, of course, only the private value of fuel economy; there are externalities, too.

(b) Other applications
There are various other applications of microelectronics in cars. A continuously variable transmission could make an even more significant contribution to fuel economy. Naturally, there are severe mechanical problems here, but microprocessor control would be an essential part of the system. Some estimates suggest that such a system could lead to fuel savings of more like 20 per cent.

Diagnostic systems and vehicle condition monitoring require a certain amount of (not very complex) electronics. The major problem here is making the necessary electromechanical sensors. Brake control and anti-skid devices are control systems of some complexity, but again it is the necessary sensors that are difficult and expensive to make. Finally, car manufacturers have found some uses for microelectronics in instrumentation.

Quality required of microelectronic components

(a) Reliability
The car is one of the worst environments in which electronics is to be found, worse even than for some military equipment (see Noyce and Barrett, 1979; *Economist*, 1 March 1980). The major problems are severe electrical and magnetic transients; severe thermal conditions and thermal cycles (for example, $-40°C$ to $+125°C$, and 7,000 thermal cycles per lifetime); severe mechanical stress; severe climatic stress, including humidity (up to 100 per cent), salt, sulphur and oil. These all contribute to vastly increased failure rates (see Noyce and Barrett, 1979; Birch, 1982).

The American car industry has been very demanding about the reliability of microelectronic components. Indeed, some semiconductor engineers consider that those in the car industry are unrealistic about the reliability they require. Typically, a system of 10^4–10^5 components is expected to have a maximum failure rate of 10^{-6} fails per hour. That is a maximum failure rate per component of 10^{-10}–10^{-11} fails per hour. Such figures are readily attainable with 1980s' technology in a good environment (see Chapter 4), but if reliability rates are perhaps 100–1,000 times worse in the car environment, then 10^{-10} is ambitious by 1980s' standards.

Greater reliability can be achieved by using the CMOS technology; it may be more expensive than the nMOS and HMOS technologies, but it is less sensitive to the bad environment. Moreover, high reliability versions of standard technologies have been produced for space, military, aerospace and medical applications, but they are typically very expensive.

(b) Speed
The car is a 'real-time' system—recall Chapter 3. Every 10 milliseconds or so, an ignition pulse is due and has to be dealt with as it arises. For

applications such as fuel injection and spark control, a programme cycle has to be completed every 5–10 milliseconds. For other applications such as instrumentation and diagnostics, there is more time.

Depending on the number and speed of the sensors which are connected to the microprocessor, and the resolution (in bits) required for the engine measurements, it would seem that microprocessors for engine control may need to carry out elementary instructions in 2.5–5 microseconds. Such speeds were not attainable on the early 4-bit microprocessors, but were possible with some of the later 8-bit microprocessors (1976 onwards), and present no difficulties for 1980s' technology.

Some engine measurements must be accurate to ± 1 per cent, and if the variable in question has a dynamic range of 50:1, that calls for 12 bits resolution. This means that double precision arithmetic would be needed if an 8-bit microprocessor were used. Such operations put extra demands on the speed of the microprocessor.

(c) Capacity
Multifunction engine control needs about 100,000 transistors, while simple carburettor control systems may only have 20,000 transistors (see Noyce and Barrett, 1979). This presents no problems for present technology (see Chapter 4); the 100,000 transistors are the equivalent of about 4–6 modest integrated circuits.

In prototype and early engine control systems, a typical arrangement would involve a standard microprocessor, external ROM (1–2 KBytes), and an external input/output chip. Later versions have been based on a single-chip microcomputer. The most advanced engine control systems have used a standard, medium-performance microprocessor, 8 KBytes of ROM, and some customized components for input/output and other functions (Noyce and Barrett, 1979).

For other applications such as braking control and instrumentation, a medium-performance, single-chip microcomputer (containing 20,000–30,000 transistors) will suffice.

(d) Power consumption
All the 'production' electronic engine control systems have used some sort of MOS technology. Power consumption, even for the most sophisticated systems, is no more than a few watts. In proportion to the car battery capacity (about 0.5 kWh) and the power required by the headlights, for example, such power consumption is small, if not trivial.

(e) Size

The early experimental 'computer-controlled' car carried a minicomputer in the boot. Modern, microprocessor-based systems are sufficiently compact to fit into the cramped engine compartment.

(f) Cost

It was suggested that the private value of fuel savings from microprocessor engine control might be $200 per annum. The chips would cost no more than $20–40 (*Electronics*, 6 October 1981, pp. 139–41), but with sensors and actuators the total cost may be $400 or more (*EDN*, 7 January, 1981, pp. 61–7).

Other economic issues concerning the use of microelectronics

(a) American fuel economy and emission regulations

The main American car manufacturers have been looking at the possible use of digital electronics for engine control since the 1960s. The necessary techniques are now well understood, yet some manufacturers have indicated that they would be happier to work with the crude electromechanical controls that they are used to. These electromechanical devices would 'degrade gracefully', while digital electronics can break down catastrophically.

One reason why electronics has been introduced despite these reservations is that the American Government passed strict regulations on emissions and fuel consumption. By 1978, cars had to achieve a minimum of 18 miles per gallon, rising to a minimum of 22 miles per gallon in 1981. According to McDermott (1978), unburnt hydrocarbon emissions were to fall from 15 grams per mile in 1978 to 0.4 grams per mile in 1981, carbon monoxide emissions from 15 grams per mile to 3.4 grams per mile, and oxides of nitrogen from 2 grams per mile to 1 gram per mile.

These figures can be achieved if the air to fuel ratio is kept within strict limits, the so-called stoichometric region. This is, however, a very difficult control problem, and it is generally acknowledged that it could not be achieved without electronic engine control (*Economist*, 1 March 1980, 'Microelectronics Survey').

(b) Sensors and actuators

Compared to mechanical and electromechanical devices, semiconductors are very sensitive to noise and voltage transients. Some of the sensors that were used with electromechanical devices are too noisy to be used with semiconductors, unless modified. Similarly, some of the actuators require considerable current to drive them.

The problems can be and have been overcome, but solutions are costly. One manufacturer remarked that it was a case of the 'tail wagging the dog' (*Electronics*, 18 April 1974, p. 65): microelectronic engine control can require alterations to sensors and actuators that pose altogether greater problems than the design of the electronics!

(c) European and Japanese cars

For some time the cars made by European and Japanese manufacturers have achieved better fuel economy than American cars. The main reason is that they are smaller, lighter and often lower-performance cars than those made by American manufacturers. Indeed, many European and Japanese cars can meet the American regulations without using any electronics.

It is not surprising, therefore, that American manufacturers were the first to use microelectronics in cars. Nevertheless, Japanese consumption of automotive electronics at $1.3bn. in 1983 was not that far short of American consumption at $1.9bn. (*Electronics*, 12 January 1984).

(d) Other issues

The PSI study of microprocessors in manufactured products (Northcott, 1980) suggests that the British car industry has made relatively little use of electronics because of adverse management attitudes, and the fact that only a small proportion of engineers in the industry are electronic engineers.

A short history of microelectronics in cars[2]

In 1973, Ford started a pilot run of computerized engine control using a PDP–11 minicomputer. At about the same time, General Motors' series of computer-controlled 'cars of the future' used a minicomputer stored in the boot. These systems experimented with electronic ignition and spark control, electronic fuel injection, instrumentation, braking control, amongst other functions. Chrysler, meanwhile, had developed some of their main engine control techniques by 1974, and had a pilot run of spark control in 1975–76.

The first production microprocessor-based spark control system was the General Motors' Misar system, introduced in one 1977 model. The

Table 8.1   Summary of the man microprocessor-based engine control systems

System	Manufacturer	Date	Spark control	EGR	CLC of A:F ratio	EFI	Idle speed	Canister purge	Secondary air flow	Transmission control	Others
Misar	GM	1977	✓	—	—	—	—	—	—	—	—
EEC-I	Ford	1978	✓	✓	—	—	—	—	—	—	—
Spark Control Computer	Chrysler	1978/9	✓	✓	✓	—	—	—	—	—	—
EEC-II	Ford	1979	✓	✓	✓	—	✓	✓	✓	✓	—
CCC	GM	1979	✓	✓	✓	—	—	—	—	—	—
MCU-A	Ford	1980	—	—	✓	✓	—	—	—	—	—
—	BL	1980	—	—	—	✓	—	—	—	—	—
Bordcomputer	BMW	1980	✓	—	✓	✓	—	—	—	—	—
EEC-III	Ford	1980/1	✓	✓	✓	—	—	✓	✓	✓	—
Spark Control Computer (upgraded)	Chrysler	1981	✓	✓	✓	—	—	—	✓	—	—
ECCS	Nissan	1981/2	✓	✓	✓	✓	✓	✓	✓	✓	—
GMCM	GM	1981/2	✓	✓	✓	—	✓	✓	✓	✓	—
TCCS	Toyota	1982	✓	—	—	✓	—	✓	—	✓	Knock sensing

EGR = exhaust gas recirculation
CLC = closed-loop control
A:F ratio = air to fuel ratio
EFI = electronic fuel injection)

system computed optimum spark timing from engine speed, manifold pressure and crankshaft position. The system used Rockwell's custom-designed, 10-bit pMOS microprocessor.[3] A new computation for spark advance and dwell would be made every 12 milliseconds. With a program cycle of 335 instructions, each taking at least 10–20 microseconds, this was presumably a demanding piece of design.

Chrysler's first system, introduced in 1978, used a standard 8-bit CMOS microprocessor (RCA 1802) to control spark timing, the air to fuel ratio, and exhaust gas recirculation (EGR). The CMOS processor was somewhat faster than the pMOS processor used by General Motors, with elementary instruction times of 2–4 microseconds. This would more than compensate for the occasional need to carry out double precision calculations. Ford's first microprocessor-based control system was also introduced in 1978. Table 8.1 summarizes the main systems introduced by 1982.

Subsequent control systems have made use of more powerful microprocessors to control further engine functions. Thus, for example, General Motors' 1979 CCC system used a standard 8-bit HMOS microprocessor (Motorola 6802) to control a whole range of functions (see Table 8.1). At the same time, Ford introduced an improved system based on a custom-manufactured, 12-bit microprocessor. The 1981/82 GMCM system from General Motors uses a modified 16-bit microprocessor (Motorola 67002). By the end of 1981, almost all General Motors cars, and about 70 per cent of Chrysler cars, had microprocessors control.

There has been rather less use of microelectronics in European cars. BL and BMW introduced microprocessor control of fuel injection into some of their 'quality' cars in 1980, but microprocessor control is not widespread in standard cars. Japanese manufacturers have produced engine control systems which are comparable to those of American manufacturers, and these systems are in widespread use. The control systems used by Nissan and Toyota are described in Table 8.1.[4]

Summary and conclusion

To what extent have quality innovations in microelectronics led to increased use of microprocessors in engine control? Undoubtedly, the car environment makes considerable demands on the reliability of microelectronic components, and the use of microelectronics has to some extent been constrained by reliability. It is unlikely that the components of the early 1970s were good enough. In the same way, the car is a 'real-time' system, and some of the early pMOS microprocessors were barely fast enough to cope with engine control. By 1977, however, processor speed was not really a constraint.

The most complex control systems require about 100,000 transistors. With the technology of the late 1970s, this is no more than a few chips. The capacity of available components was not, therefore, a constraint on the application of microelectronics. Likewise, microelectronic components are very compact and very frugal; size and power dissipation did not act as constraints either.

Apart from the matter of reliability, then, the application of microelectronics in engine control was not really held back by the quality of the microelectronic components. Nevertheless, even if the technology did not hold back the application, car manufacturers have not been slow to exploit further advances in microelectronic technology. In this sense, there is a demand for improved qualities.

As already suggested, if anything has held back the application of microelectronics in engine control, it is the development of suitable sensors and actuators. Early versions of these devices were quite satisfactory for use with mechanical control systems, but not with the rather more sensitive electronic systems. In some cases these sensors and actuators have been difficult and expensive to make: the application of electronics requires changes in the associated components which present a greater design problem than the electronic system itself.

Moreover, any discussion of developments in microprocessor engine control would be incomplete without reference to the United States' Government fuel economy and emissions standards. Such standards have subtle implications for innovative activity, but it seems unlikely that microprocessor engine control would have taken place as soon as it did without the United States' Government's involvement.

8.2 Microelectronics in telephone exchanges

Applications

There are two types of electronic telephone exchange: the 'quasi-electronic' and the 'fully electronic'. To understand the difference between them, it helps to understand the electromechanical systems they replaced. The earliest form of electromechanical exchange was the Strowger system.[5] This was first used at the end of the nineteenth century, but it has continually been refined, and it is still in widespread use today (see the 'short history' below, section (d)). Here the control and switching functions are integrated in decentralized units. This makes for reliability as any one unit can break down without disturbing the others, except in the sense of increasing their workload. The system is very slow, however.

In the 1940s, a completely different electromechanical system—the Crossbar—was introduced in the United States. This uses a system of 'common control', where the control and switching functions are separated, and control is centralized. This system is more amenable to the introduction of electronic control, for such developments could take place quite independently of advances in switching technology. The system is economical in terms of equipment, and fast.

The 'quasi-electronic' systems are crossbar systems with electronic control, but still using electromechanical switching.[6] The electronic control system may involve 'stored program control', or they may be 'hard-wired', as defined in Section 3.1. The stored program control systems are inherently more flexible than the hard-wired.

The 'fully electronic' system has electronic control and electronic switching. The switching of analog signals by digital electronic circuitry is a rather inefficient operation, and consequently electronic switching almost invariably means the switching of digital signals. Ordinary speech is converted to a digital form by the technique of pulse coded modulation (PCM). Such fully electronic exchanges would almost invariably use stored program control.

Quality required of microelectronic components

(a) The meaning of reservation qualities
For the telecommunications authority setting up a completely new telecommunications system, the electronic exchange will look attractive if it dominates the earlier electromechanical systems. Thus, the quality required of the microelectronic components is whatever it takes to make the electronic exchange dominate electromechanical systems. The quality of earlier electromechanical systems defines the 'reservation quality'.

For the authority considering whether to replace an existing and working system with a new system, the calculation is rather different. The electronic system must be of considerably higher quality to justify the costs of replacement. To be precise, the discounted incremental benefits from the higher quality system must exceed the replacement cost. Thus the reservation quality depends on whether the system is a new system or a replacement system.

The analysis of Section 2.4 is relevant here. We saw there how quality choice and timing of purchase for a durable good depends on expected future quality innovation and price reductions. In Figure 2.3, timing depends on the slopes of the indifference curves and intertemporal budget constraints. We would argue that the indifference curves are much steeper for the buyer of a new system than for the buyer of a replacement system. Loosely speaking, the 'disutility' of delay for the buyer of a new system is that he has no system in the meantime; for the buyer of a replacement system, the 'disutility' is simply the incremental quality foregone. The buyer of a new system would require a very rapid rate of quality innovation to justify delaying purchase, hence the steep indifference curve; the buyer of a replacement system needs only a rather more modest rate of quality innovation to justify postponing replacement, hence the flat indifference curve.

The illustrative example in Section 2.4 showed how it is difficult to infer much about static reservation prices from paid prices when buyers delay purchases in expectation of future price reductions. The same holds for reservation qualities. All we attempt to do, therefore, is to describe some of the improvements in telephone exchanges that can follow from the use of electronics.

(b) High quality microelectronic exchanges
The electronic exchanges that have been made are superior to electro-mechanical systems in most respects. In terms of size, a 1960 crossbar system's memory unit was about fifty times more bulky than the 1975 microelectronic equivalent.[7] Likewise, Bell Labs' first fully electronic exchange (ESS No. 4) had five times the capacity of its immediate electromechanical predecessor, but took up only a quarter of the space; the replacement of magnetic core by semiconductor memory and the use of microprocessors more than halved the dimensions of the ESS No. 4.

In terms of speed, the common control system is faster than the Strowger system in any case, but electronic control increased the performance of crossbar systems by a factor of four. Moreover, the electromechanical switching devices are very slow compared to semiconductors.

Electromechanical components consume a lot more power than electronic components. Stored program control offers much more flexibility than electromechanical control, and offers far more scope for improved telecommunications systems.[8] Finally, digital transmission is much less noisy than analog transmission.

(c) Electronic exchanges before microelectronics

Electronic vacuum tubes (valves) consumed much too much power and were insufficiently reliable for electronic exchange control; experimental systems using valves were not a success (see below). The advent of transistors, however, and the introduction of redundancy in design made electronic exchanges much more reliable than electromechanical exchanges.

The decentralized control of the Strowger system meant that even if any individual unit was not too reliable, the system as a whole was rather reliable. Semiconductors are inherently much more reliable than electromechanical devices, but with centralized control a single failure is rather more serious. Redundancy in design is the engineer's way of making such failures less serious.

The value of reliability should not be underestimated; Bessant *et al.* (1980) show that the increased reliability of microelectronic exchanges made for substantially reduced maintenance costs.[9] Some have suggested, however, that the British Post Office had an unnecessary obsession with reliability, and made unrealistic demands on component reliability.

Other economic issues

(a) Pure diffusion?

Experiments with electronic telephone exchanges began in the 1950s, but it is known that as early as 1936 researchers at Bell Labs had come to the view that mechanical relays in telephone exchanges would have to be replaced by electronic connections in due course (Braun and MacDonald, 1978). They were aware that the growing complexity of the telephone system, and the greater demands that would be made of it, would require a more flexible system of control. As valves were not at that time a suitable technology, it would appear that Bell Labs had in mind some improved form of valve technology, if not a radical form of electronic technology. Indeed, the discovery of the transistor in the late 1940s[10] was in a sense the result of a desire to improve telephone exchange technology.

In short, the idea of electronic telephone exchanges is as old as the transistor itself; it would seem that 'pure' diffusion is not at work here. Nevertheless, there remains a problem of communication between the telephone engineer and the semiconductor engineer, since they speak a rather different language (Falk, 1977). This language barrier and the telephone engineer's familiarity with electromechanical systems is often cited as reasons why the use of microelectronics in telephone exchanges did not progress as fast as it might have done.

(b) Development times

Electronic exchanges have required very long development times. The first of Bell Labs' electronic telephone exchanges is thought to be the largest single development project ever undertaken at Bell Labs; five years elapsed between the first trial of stored program control and the completion of the project, while nine years elapsed between the first trial of an electronic control office and the project's completion. In the United Kingdom, work on the TXE4A dates to spring 1975, but the system was first installed in 1981—a development time of six years. The TXE4 was first planned in 1963, and given a trial from 1969 to 1972, but it was not introduced until 1976.[11]

The components used at design stage tend to be 'proven technology', which means that they may be some five years beyond introduction. With a development lag of five years or more, the components used will be some ten years beyond introduction, and thus somewhat outdated. For example, the components used in TXE4 were discrete, since integrated circuits did not appear in volume until the mid-1960s; by the date of introduction of TXE4 in 1976, however, the 'state of the art' technology was the microprocessor, not the discrete component.

A similar picture emerges for the British Post Office's System X. Development work started in 1976 and made use of the early 1970s' technology—medium-scale integration in TTL and CMOS. When the first System X exchange was introduced in 1980, it was based on outdated (if not exactly obsolete) technology. This observation is made simply in order to demonstrate the folly of trying to correlate current developments in telephone exchanges with contemporary developments in microelectronics.

(c) Growth of digital traffic

Early telephone traffic was entirely analog, but since the 1960s, a small but growing proportion of the traffic has been naturally digital. That is to say, it is the output from or input to computer systems; examples are Prestel and Electronic Mail. Currently, the digital signal is modified to an analog form for transmission over an analog line, but transmission over a digital line would be easier.

The growth in digital traffic will make the digital telephone line the natural method of transmission. This growth can be assessed from the following figures on 'network termination points' (NTPs) based on Beesley (1981):

	NTPs (1,000s)			NTPs/1,000 handsets
	1972	1979	1987 forecast	1979
UK	32	120	380	5
USA	500	2000	—	12

The NTPs per 1,000 handsets figure is a slightly misleading measure of the proportion of traffic that is digital because NTPs make heavier use of the system than ordinary handsets. Beesley (1981. p. 10) estimates that the proportion of British telecommunications revenue coming from digital traffic was about 6 per cent in 1979.

(d) Government constraints
Finally, the use of microelectronics in British telecommunications systems has been constrained by the British Government's reluctance to allow imports of exchange equipment, and their requirement that domestic exchange equipment be designed around British-manufactured components—a striking example of the difficulties that this can cause is given in Scar and Swindle (1978).

Evidence presented to the Post Office Review Committee in 1977 suggested that the Post Office had particular requirements for the design of telephone exchange equipment that made the equipment of limited interest to export markets.[12]

A short history of electronic telephone exchanges[13]

(a) Prototype systems
Bell Labs first experimented with electronic control of telephone exchanges in 1956, and a stored program control system had its first trial in 1960. The experimental systems were based on valves and, as we mentioned before, these components were unsuitable. These systems were also fully electronic, but that proved to be too difficult, and

subsequent development effort was on quasi-electronic systems. Indeed, the only part of the system to emerge unscathed from the trial was the concept of stored program control.

The British Post Office started research into electronic switching in the late 1940s, and an experimental fully electronic exchange (Highgate Wood) was opened in 1962. The system was mainly based on valves, like the Bell Labs system, and for that reason did not go beyond the experimental stage. Similar experiments with fully electronic exchanges took place in other countries at about the same time, but in all cases the conclusion was that the quasi-electronic system was the appropriate design for the 1960s.

(b) The first systems in public service

The first electronic exchange in public service was the Bell Labs No.1 ESS, introduced in 1965. This was a quasi-electronic system, using stored program control and ferreed crosspoint switches. A typical system would handle 10,000 lines, and required some 300,000 semiconductors: 70,000 transistors, 130,000 logic diodes and 100,000 other semiconductors. The control circuitry would carry out elementary instructions in 5.5 microseconds, and the memory was magnetic core.

The United Kingdom's first electronic exchange, the TXE2, followed in 1966. It was similar in many respects, but did not use stored program control. Like the No.1 ESS, it was based on transistors and diodes, and used reed relays for switching. To begin with it was only designed to work as a small exchange (200–2,000 lines), but later versions were able to handle 7,000 lines. It was followed by the much larger TXE4 in 1976, which was still based on discrete components, and still made no use of stored program control. A modified version of the TXE4 (the TXE4–A), introduced in 1981, used some integrated circuits and stored program control.

By 1970 there were electronic exchanges with stored program control in Sweden, Japan, France, Canada, Australia and the Netherlands. By about 1974, such systems had been introduced in West Germany and in Eastern Europe. But as the Carter Report noted with some concern, there was not one stored program control system in the United Kingdom by 1977.

(c) Fully electronic exchanges

Although the experiments of the early 1960s had not been a success, work to develop fully electronic exchanges resumed in the late 1960s.

The first large, fully electronic exchange was the Bell Labs No. 4 ESS, introduced in 1976. This system would deal with digital signals only, which makes electronic switching feasible. The exchange handles 500,000 calls per hour.

There has subsequently been a continuing process of evolution in the design of the No. 4 ESS: the modularity of design makes small adjustments possible and worthwhile. Some of the improvements have been: the replacement of magnetic core memory by MOS RAM (random access memory); the use of microprocessors for some peripheral applications; the increased use of LSI (large scale integrated) components; and, of particular importance, steady improvements in the control software.

Development work on the British Post Office's System X started in 1976, and the first exchange was introduced in 1980. Again it is a modular system, and while some nMOS microprocessors are used, the exchange mainly uses MSI (medium-scale integration) TTL and CMOS components; these components were first introduced in about 1970.

(d) The replacement of electromechanical exchanges

The replacement of existing electromechanical exchanges has been, and will continue to be, a slow process. Moreover, the replacement exchanges are not necessarily the most recent designs. In 1980–81, for example, British Telecom authorized expenditures of £30m on Strowger equipment, £24m on the TXE2, £225m on the TXE4 and TXE4–A, but only £6m on System X (British Telecom).

By 1979, about 20 per cent of Strowger exchanges had been replaced, though less than half of the replacement equipment were quasi-electronic or electronic exchanges (PO Telecommunications Statistics). A similar picture emerges in most other countries. By that date, no country except the United States had a substantial proportion of electronic exchanges. The main difference between countries is that some (Sweden, France, Japan and the United States) have replaced a large proportion of Strowger exchanges by the intermediate crossbar exchange; others (United Kingdom and West Germany) have not (Bessant *et al.*, 1980).

Summary and conclusion

To what extent has quality innovation in microelectronic components led to an increased use of electronic telephone exchanges? While valve technology was not satisfactory for electronic telephone exchanges, the first quasi-electronic exchanges which used discrete transistors were an improvement on the earlier electromechanical exchanges in terms of reliability, speed, power consumption, flexibility, and size. Exchanges built around integrated circuits offered even greater improvements. Nevertheless, the replacement of electromechanical exchanges by improved electronic exchanges has, not surprisingly perhaps, been a slow process.

If further quality innovation is expected, replacement of a working system is liable to be postponed. It is not a matter of the underlying microelectronic technology not being good enough. Moreover, further improvements in microelectronics are not essential to bring about widespread use of electronic exchanges. In this sense there is not a strong demand for further quality improvements. Nevertheless, improvements in microelectronic technology are exploited, even if the long development times mean that the components used in a new exchange are some five to ten years behind the 'state of the art'.

For countries such as the United Kingdom where most of the existing equipment is of the earliest electromechanical design (Strowger), replacement is complicated by the fact that the electronic exchanges have very different methods of operation, and it is difficult to operate the two together. Moreover, it is suggested that the development and installation of electronic exchanges has been held back by a 'language barrier' between telephone engineers and semiconductor manufacturers, and in some cases by governments' reluctance to allow imports of exchange equipment or components. It is thought, however, that the growth of digital traffic on telephone lines will increase the value of fully electronic telephone exchanges.

8.3 Microelectronics in calculators

Applications

The mechanical calculating machine dates to the seventeenth century when Pascal and Leibnitz designed machines to compute the four arithmetic functions. Such machines were not really automatic, in the sense that frequent operator intervention was required. Babbage was the first to describe an automatic calculating machine, with which more complex functions could be evaluated but, as is well known, he was not able to build a working model of his design (Hollingdale and Toothill, 1970).

Mechanical calculators never really progressed beyond the non-automatic stage. For complex calculations with a non-automatic calculator, the limiting factor is not so much the time taken for elementary calculations, but the operator's time. In a sense, therefore, the four-function pocket calculator is not as significant an advance as the programmable or scientific calculator; the ability to add two numbers in ever fewer milliseconds is less important than the ability to carry out sequences of calculations automatically.

The electronic calculator is one of the most 'electronic' of products, with electronic components accounting for a large proportion of manufacturing costs. Valery (1975) gives a breakdown of the cost of a scientific calculator in 1975. Two points emerge from his estimates. First, the integrated circuits and other electronic components account for more than a half of manufacturing costs, though for a simple four-function calculator the integrated circuit would have been a smaller proportion of manufacturing cost. Moreover, while all the costs have fallen over time, the integrated circuit cost has fallen most rapidly. As a proportion of manufacturing costs, therefore, the cost of the integrated circuit has fallen since then. Second, manufacturing cost was less than a third of the retail price, although at the time the pricing of scientific calculators was not very competitive—much less so than the pricing of four-function calculators.

Quality required of microelectronic components

We shall see that the electronic calculator is a very good example of 'waiting for the technology to be good enough'. This becomes clear when we see how and why the premature attempts to make electronic calculators failed. It will also become clear that those calculators which represented the 'leading edge' could only be made by stretching the technology to its limit.

(a) Component density

The major obstacle for the pocket calculator was the problem of trying to manufacture an integrated circuit containing a sufficient number of transistors. There were no valve calculators to speak of, and since even the simplest calculator requires many hundreds of transistors, the calculators made of discrete transistors were 'desk-top' rather than 'pocket'.

The first attempt to manufacture an integrated circuit calculator was in 1965—the Victor Comptometer Corporation's Victor 3900.[14] The design used twenty-nine pMOS integrated circuits with hundreds of transistors per chip. Such component densities were very high by 1965 standards (see Chapter 4), and it was not surprising when the chip manufacturers obtained an extremely low yield of working chips. In terms of the simple model of Section 3.5, the design failed because the manufacturer attempted to push the technology too far, and put too much capacity on to a single chip too soon. The calculator never appeared.

In 1972, one American firm (Ragen) tried to produce a four-function calculator on a single chip, using the CMOS technology. At that time the CMOS transistor was about twice as large as the pMOS transistor, so that a larger chip area was required for the same transistor capacity. The resulting chip had an area of 28 square millimetres, which was very large by 1972 standards, and once again the manufacturers were unable to obtain satisfactory yields. In the 'short history' below, we shall discuss some successful attempts to manufacture pocket calculators.

(b) Power consumption

The development of technologies with low power consumption has also been essential to the successful manufacture of the pocket calculator. The first CMOS technology appeared in 1968 (see Chapter 4), but the important 'silicon gate' CMOS appeared in 1971. The early CMOS calculator chips required about 2 milliwatts, while the comparable pMOS chip would require 100 milliwatts, or more.[15] At the same time, even the pMOS integrated circuit would consume less power than the light-emitting diode (LED) display, for which 200 milliwatts is a typical power dissipation. The true value of the CMOS technology was not exploited until the development of the very frugal liquid crystal display (LCD) in the mid-1970s.

(c) Speed and reliability

As mentioned above, speed of operation is hardly very important for the four-function calculator. For the scientific calculator, however, speed could matter. For example, in the design of the Hewlett Packard HP–35, the designers wanted a maximum computation time of one second for any function (Whitney *et al.*, 1972; *Electronics*, 1 February 1975). This called for a 200 kilohertz clock speed, which was fast for low power pMOS, but manageable. Since the introduction of the HP–35 in 1972, power-delay products have fallen (Figures 4.1–4.3), so that such speeds can easily be achieved at very low levels of power dissipation.

In the same way, reliability improvements are not important here. It is typically the moving parts—keys, switches, etc.—which would fail first. At 1970 failure rates (Section 4.3), the calculator chip with a thousand transistors would have a mean-time between failure of 300–400 years!

Other economic issues

For the production of calculator chips and their incorporation into finished calculators, there are not really any other issues. As we mentioned above, it is essentially a matter of 'waiting for the technology to be good enough', especially for the chip designs commissioned by calculator manufacturers. The calculator has a relatively short design and development period. The Hewlett Packard HP–35 programmable scientific calculator was designed and developed in about eighteen months (Whitney *et al.*, 1972; *Electronics*, 1 February 1975); for simple four-function calculators, development periods are much shorter.

For the end-user, however, there is some 'pure' diffusion; as one industry observer put it (quoted in Braun and MacDonald, 1978), people did not know they needed pocket calculators until they had them. Moreover, as a durable good which (from casual empiricism) is replaced every four years or so, the calculator is a good example to be analyzed by the simple model of Section 2.4. Indeed, the calculator is one of the most striking early examples of consumers postponing their first purchase in anticipation of price reductions and quality improvements; first purchases might only take place when the price had fallen well below the static reservation price as defined in Section 2.4.

A short history of microelectronics in calculators[16]

(a) Pre-microelectronic calculators
As mentioned before, there were no valve calculators to speak of; they were too large and consumed too much power. The first electronic calculators were introduced in 1962, and used discrete transistors. The early calculators had very many separate components, and assembly costs were substantial.

(b) Four-function calculators
We have already described the first (unsuccessful) attempt to make a calculator with integrated circuits. The first successful four-function

calculator was made in 1968 by the Japanese company Hayakawa using American-manufactured bipolar integrated circuits. A year later, four-function calculators made from MOS components started to appear. At that time, assembly costs were still a fairly large proportion of total costs.

In 1970, the first small desk-top calculator appeared. It made use of a set of six chips from the company Electronic Arrays. Later in the same year, Canon and Texas Instruments together introduced an 'almost pocket' calculator based on three chips.

The first integrated circuits to contain all the calculator functions on one chip were made by Mostek and Texas Instruments in 1971. The Mostek design had to be very economical with components (2,100 transistors), and it was only just possible to integrate all functions on to a chip of 21 square millimetres. Various manufacturers (Canon and Texas Instruments) had designed pocket calculators around these chips by early 1972.

The first attempt to make a CMOS calculator was, as we saw before, unsuccessful. The first successful attempt was a two-chip design by Sharp, introduced in 1972.

(c) Scientific and programmable calculators
The first scientific calculator was the Hewlett Packard HP–35, introduced in 1972. From an early stage in the development of the product, it became clear to the designers that the greatest challenge would be the design and development of the MOS integrated circuits. The design makes use of five integrated circuits, containing a total of more than 10,000 gates. Two of the chips were larger than 20 square millimetres, which was about the limit in 1972. It appears, then, that Hewlett Packard were pushing the technology about as far as they could to achieve the required density. Indeed, it is said that they had to opt for the 'reverse polish logic' in the keystroke routines because the integrated circuits simply could not contain the extra circuitry required for the possibly more familiar 'algebraic logic' (Whitney *et al.*, 1972).

Hewlett Packard have produced many improved versions of this calculator which took advantage of the quality innovation in micro-electronic components. In 1974, they introduced the first hand-held programmable calculator, with magnetic card storage. With 51 key functions and capable of handling programs of up to 100 steps, it compared favourably with 'desk-top' programmable calculators.

From 1976 onwards, many other manufacturers started to introduce

ever-more powerful programmable calculators, with ever-more functions and program steps. By 1981, the most elaborate programmable
calculators are comparable to the smallest microcomputers, such as the
Sharp pocket computer. Indeed, the distinction between a pocket computer and a calculator is rapidly becoming blurred, but if a distinction
remains it is that the computer can be programmed in a high-level
language, while the calculator is programmed in something more like a
machine code.

Summary and conclusion

To what extent has quality innovation in microelectronics increased the
use of microelectronics in this application? For this case study, the
answer is very easy: the use of microelectronics is almost entirely
determined by quality innovation. The date at which the early electronic
calculators were introduced was simply determined by the date at which
the underlying microelectronic technology was good enough. Moreover,
calculator manufacturers have been very quick to exploit further quality
innovation in the components.

When analyzing the demand from the end-user, however, it is likely
that there is an element of 'pure' diffusion, and moreover that purchases
are postponed to take advantage of expected quality innovation.

8.4 A summary

The purpose of these case studies has been to describe the extent to
which quality innovation in microelectronic components has led to a
greater demand for microelectronics in the particular application.
Naturally, it would be foolish to generalize from this sample of three;
different case studies could yield quite different conclusions.[17] What the
case studies can do, however, is give us a broader perspective on the
many issues that have to be resolved before microelectronics can and
will be used for a particular application.

The use of microelectronics in car engine control has, in a narrow
sense, grown as the quality of microelectronic components has
improved. The aspect of quality that is of particular importance here is
the reliability of components. The car is a particularly bad environment
for the reliable functioning of electronic components. In a more sympathetic environment, standard components would be quite reliable
enough for what is not a particularly complex control system, but in this

environment reliability has been a constraint on the application of microelectronics. As semiconductor manufacturers have resolved the reliability problem, so the demand for microelectronic components has grown.

The case study found that various other aspects of quality required for the operation of a real-time system of this sort were not really binding constraints. If anything, indeed, the most important constraint on the use of microelectronics was not the quality of the microelectronic components themselves, but the quality and cost of the associated electro-mechanical sensors and actuators.

The conclusion is that while improvements in the quality of the microelectronic components are exploited to provide more flexible or more powerful systems, many of these improvements are not (with the exception of reliability improvements) essential for the successful use of microelectronics in engine control.

The case study of the use of microelectronics in telephone exchanges came to a similar conclusion. The first quasi-electronic exchanges built from discrete transistors represent a considerable advance on earlier electromechanical exchanges, and those built from integrated circuits represent an even greater advance. Nevertheless, the replacement of electromechanical exchanges by electronic exchanges has been a slow process in most countries.

The conclusion is that while quality improvements in the microelectronic components are exploited in the design of telephone exchanges, further quality improvements are not necessary to make the electronic exchange a worthwhile replacement. Indeed, in keeping with the simple model of Section 2.4, it would appear that part of the reason why the replacement of exchanges has been a slow process is precisely that telecommunications authorities are postponing replacement in anticipation of further quality advances.

The case study of microelectronics in calculators is rather different. The development of the pocket calculator was, at least until the mid-1970s, constrained by the quality of the microelectronic technology. Some premature attempts to make smaller calculators failed simply because the manufacturer had attempted to push the technology too far. Many of the successful products were only just technically feasible at their date of introduction. Moreover, further advances in the technology have been exploited very rapidly with steady improvements in the performance and capacity of advanced calculators.

For the end-user, however, there is a suggestion of 'pure' diffusion, and it seems likely that demand (especially replacement demand) can be postponed in anticipation of future quality innovation.

The implications for the theory of demand the theory of innovation are simple. These results do not necessarily make the static analysis of choice between a variety of qualities invalid. The results do imply, however, that it would in general be misleading to attempt to explain the growth in demand for microelectronics simply in terms of the observed quality innovation. Moreover, any simple relationship of that sort is complicated by the fact that a rapid rate of innovation may lead to postponement of demand.

These conclusions are in line with some other case-study evidence. The Policy Studies Institute have carried out a number of studies of the use of microelectronics in production processes and finished products.[18] Northcott (1980) studied the use of microelectronic components in finished products, and found few instances where the components were of insufficient quality. Moreover, he emphasized that:

The bewilderingly rapid pace of change in microelectronics technology and the wide choice of different chips now available is inevitably confusing to companies new to this field, and causes some of them to have difficulty deciding which is the most appropriate integrated circuit to use . . . when new developments around the corner may soon make the chip they have used obsolete (p.19).

In a later survey, Northcott (1982) found that about 9 per cent of establishments surveyed made reference to 'very important' technical difficulties with microelectronic components (p. 50), but in many cases this was the problem of choosing from the rapidly changing available range. Nevertheless, a small number of users complained that there was no component suitable for their application, that the components were unreliable or faulty, or that the latest models were not available early enough in Britain.

This survey also suggests that technical difficulties with microprocessors were less common than difficulties with electromechanical sensors and software.

After reviewing eight detailed case studies of the use of microelectronics,[19] Lund *et al.* (1980, p. 156) concluded that 'The major technical constraints to the use of microprocessors in products and equipment appear . . . to involve related technologies rather than the electronics themselves'. They concede, however, that this may be a result of selection bias since 'failures' were not studied.

Notes

1. This is just an illustrative calculation, assuming an implicit payback period of two years.
2. The main sources for what follows are: *Electronics*, McDermott (1978), Lund *et al.* (1980), and various papers at the 2nd International Conference on Automotive Electronics, Institution of Electrical Engineers, 1979.
3. Rockwell custom-manufactured microprocessor.
4. The Nissan System is designed around the Motorola 6802.
5. Strowger was an innovative undertaker from Kansas City who, suspecting that the telephone operators were diverting his calls to rivals and thus losing him business, devised a switching system that could not be abused in that way.
6. These would be ferreeds or reed relays.
7. The main sources for what follows are: *Bell Labs Record, Post Office Electrical Engineers Journal, Telecommunication Journal*, Braun and MacDonald (1978), *inter alia*.
8. As noted by the Carter Report (1977).
9. The move from electromechanical to quasi-electronic equipment reduced maintenance effort by 60 per cent.
10. The inventors were researchers at Bell Labs.
11. *Bell Labs Record, The Post Office Electrical Engineers Journal* (various issues).
12. Carter Report (1977), Appendix Section 5, evidence from STC.
13. The main sources for what follows are: *Bell Labs Record, Post Office Electrical Engineers Journal, Telecommunication Journal*, Cripps and Godley (1978), Kotov (1968), Braun and MacDonald (1978), *inter alia*.
14. The sources for what follows are: *Electronics, New Scientist, US Department of Commerce Report*, 'Impact of Electronics on the US Calculator Industry', 1975; Wilson *et al.* (1980), McWhorter (1976).
15. Estimates based on data in Chapter 4.
16. Sources as in note 14.
17. If this is the case, we should also be careful about any generalizations based on econometric results.
18. In addition to those mentioned is the study by Bessant (1982).
19. The case studies were: heating, ventilation and air conditioning controls; automobiles; word processing; electronic postage scales; process control; medical equipment; monitors for hydraulic cranes; sewing machines.

9 Conclusion

In this chapter we summarize the main conclusions of the study, and try to draw together their implications for our understanding of the process of quality innovation in microelectronics.

Summary

In Chapter 2, we distinguished two reinforcing effects of quality innovation on the firm's demand curve: the expansion of market demand, and the improvement in competitive position. The former happens as quality innovation shifts the price function downward and to the right; the latter happens when the convexity of the price function changes, so that consumers are drawn in towards the new quality from other adjacent qualities.

In the static context, the effect of quality innovation on demand is relatively easy to analyze. We saw that the demand for a new and improving durable good was complicated by two issues: first, the existence of 'pure' diffusion, which is the growth in demand for a good that comes about as a result of a spread of knowledge about (and understanding of) the good; second, the fact that when there is no second-hand market (or a very imperfect market), consumers may postpone the purchase of a durable good in anticipation of future quality improvements and price reductions. Quality innovation may lead to growth in market demand, but the expectation of future quality innovation can delay the growth of demand.

There are two issues in the analysis of how quality innovation affects competitive position: first, to what extent does any quality innovation strengthen a firm's market position before retaliation; second, how do rivals react to any such innovation, and to what extent do such reactions offset the effect of the original innovation? The answer to the second question depends on whether firms cluster in product space. From our discussion of the spatial and product competition literature, we found that while the original Hotelling model predicted clustering, various extensions to that model did not; we also saw that the existence of agglomeration economies provided an added incentive for clustering.

In Chapter 3, we saw that many applications of electronics could be thought of as small computer systems. We saw that there were various intrinsic relationships between the various quality parameters, and that (roughly speaking) the cost of producing quality would, beyond a certain point, increase exponentially with quality.

Chapter 4 described, in broad outline, the history of quality innovation in microelectronics from the 1960s to the present. Two particularly striking features have been the rapid decline in prices of microelectronic components, and the substantial and continuing improvements in product quality, especially in speed, power consumption, reliability and capacity. Microelectronic technology has undoubtedly been rich in technological opportunities over the period, but large research and development expenditures have been needed to realize these opportunities—as much as 10 per cent of sales revenue.

Chapter 5 showed how the quality innovation in microprocessors can be described as a series of adjustments to the price function relating price to quality. The estimation of a time series of price functions raised some quite interesting econometric issues; in particular, the procedure of estimation with undominated points. Broadly speaking, there is a downward trend in the prices of all microprocessors over the period, with the prices of higher quality products falling faster than the prices of lower quality products. We found that the econometric estimates of large dimension price functions show some instability; estimates of a smaller dimension function were a little more reliable, and we argued that because we use undominated points, these small dimension functions will not necessarily suffer from specification bias.

Chapter 6 describes the quality innovation strategies of individual producers of microprocessors. There is evidence of clustering in product space, which suggests that the competitive advantage brought about by quality innovation is to some extent eroded. Using a simple breakdown of new qualities into horizontal innovations, vertical innovations and clustering, we found very high probabilities of clustering. There are, however, significant differences between firms, and the ideas of 'coherence' and 'phase difference' are a useful way to distinguish between leaders, followers and mavericks. The observed clustering is probably an indication of important agglomeration economies.

Chapter 7 examined the changing demand for microelectronics over the period. We observed that while sales of the high quality categories may grow relatively quickly, some of these still account for only a small proportion of total sales. In addition, we reported the results of a preliminary attempt at quality demand analysis for different qualities of microprocessor. The data are too imperfect and the sample too short for the analysis to be more than exploratory. Nevertheless, the technique could be promising with more sympathetic data.

Chapter 8 reported the results of three case studies: the application of microelectronics in car engine control, telephone exchanges, and electronic calculators. In each case, we tried to assess from an engineering point of view whether the quality of available components has acted as a constraint on the development of that application. The most important thing about these case studies is that they give us a realistic perspective on the many issues that must be resolved before microelectronics can be used in a particular application. In two cases, quality innovation is not really crucial to the use of microelectronics, except perhaps in a very narrow sense; in the third, it is.

Implications

At first sight it might appear that there is a limited incentive for quality innovation. Quality innovation in microelectronic components is expensive and while one firm's innovation can increase its market share at the expense of rivals, the preponderance of clustering in quality space means that in the long run such innovations tend to be cancelled out by those of other firms. Moreover, it is not certain that there are a large number of potential consumers for whom only the highest quality will suffice.

In such circumstances the best collusive strategy might be a slower rate of quality innovation, but in a competitive environment with strong technological opportunity, the incentive for quality innovation remains. The view of many industry observers is that there is still a considerable potential for further quality innovation (Barron, 1984; Barron and Curnow, 1979; Folberth and Bleher, 1979, amongst others). Given this very considerable technological opportunity, and the expectation that competitors will try to exploit this opportunity, firms feel obliged to make use of rapid quality innovation, or else find their products rapidly becoming dominated. The incentives for staying in the race are great, because demand will grow as a result of 'pure' diffusion, even if not as a result of quality innovation.

In summary, the market incentive for quality innovations may appear some time before the end-user is able to appreciate the true value of the innovation.

Bibliography

Abbott, L. (1955) *Quality and Competition*, New York: Columbia University Press.

Aigner, D., Lovell, C. A. K. and Schmidt, P.(1977) 'Formulation and Estimation of Stochastic Frontier Production Function Models', *Journal of Econometrics*, Vol. 6, No. 1, pp. 21–37.

Aitchison, J. and Brown, J. A. C. (1957) *The Lognormal Distribution*, Cambridge: Cambridge University Press.

Aono, S. and Hata, Y. (1981) 'Microprocessor Engine Control', *Microprocessors and Microsystems*, Vol. 5, No. 10, pp. 451–7 (December).

Bain, A. D. (1962) *The Growth of Television Ownership in the U. K. since the War: A Lognormal Model*, Cambridge: University of Cambridge Department of Applied Economics, Monograph 12.

Bardon, J-P., Chanaron, J-J., Friedenson, P. and Laux, J. M. (1983) *The Automobile Revolution: The Impact of an Industry*, Chapel Hill: University of North Carolina Press.

Barron, I. (1978) 'The Future of the Microprocessor', *Microelectronics Journal*, Vol. 8, No. 4, pp. 32–6 (June).

Barron, I. (1984) 'Concurrent Silicon Systems', Lecture to the Royal Society of London, April 5.

Barron, I. and Curnow, R. (1979) *The Future with Microelectronics*, London: Frances Pinter Publishers.

Barten, A. P. (1969) 'Maximum Likelihood Estimation of a Complete System of Demand Equations', *European Economic Review*, Vol. 1, No. 1, pp. 7–73.

Beesley, M. (1981) *Liberalisation of the Use of the British Telecommunications Network*, London: HMSO.

Beizer, B. (1978) *Micro-Analysis of Computer System Performance*, New York: Van Nostrand Reinhold.

Bell Labs Record, various issues.

Bessant, J. R. (1982) *Microprocessors in Production Processes*, London: Policy Studies Institute, Report No. 609 (July).

Bessant, J. R., Bowen, J. A. E., Dickson, K. E. and Marsh, J. (1980) *The Impact of Microelectronics—a Review of the Literature*, London: Frances Pinter Publishers.

Birch, B. (1982) 'Applying Microcomputers to Vehicle Instrumentation', *Microprocessors and Microsystems*, Vol. 6, No. 7, pp. 371–77 (September).

Bloch, E. and Henle, R. A. (1968) 'Advances in Circuit Technology and their Impact on Computing Systems', in Morrell, A. J. H. (ed.), *Proceedings of the IFIP Conference* (Edinburgh, 1968), Amsterdam: North Holland.

Bonus, H. (1973) 'Quasi Engel Curves, Diffusion and the Ownership of Major Consumer Durables', *Journal of Political Economy*, Vol. 81, No. 3, pp. 655–77 (May/June).

Braun, E. and MacDonald, S. (1978) *Revolution in Miniature: The History and Impact of Semi-conductor Electronics*, Cambridge: Cambridge University Press.

Bursky, D. (1978) *Microprocessor Data Manual*, Rochelle Park, New Jersey: Hayden.

Business Week, various issues.

Carter, C. F. (1977) *Report of the Post Office Review Committee*, CMND 6850, London: HMSO (July); also *Appendix to the Report*, CMND 6954, London: HMSO (November).

Chamberlin, E. H. (1933) *The Theory of Monopolistic Competition*, Cambridge, Mass.: Harvard University Press.

Chow, G. C. (1967) 'Technological Change and the Demand for Computers', *American Economic Review*, Vol. 57, No. 5, pp. 1117–30 (December).

Clark, G. N. (1947) *The Seventeenth Century*, 2nd Edition, Oxford: Clarendon Press.

Cole, C. W. (1939) *Colbert and a Century of French Mercantilism*, Volumes I and II, New York: Columbia University Press.

Court, A. T. (1939) 'Hedonic Price Indexes with Automotive Examples', in Horner, S. L. (ed.), *The Dynamics of Automobile Demand*, New York: General Motors Corporation.

Court, L. M. (1941) 'Entrepreneurial and Consumer Demand Theories for Commodity Spectra', *Econometrica*, Vol. 9, No. 1, pp. 135–62 (April), and Vol. 9, No. 2, pp. 241–97 (July/October).

Cowling, K. and Rayner, A. J. (1970) 'Price Quality and Market Share', *Journal of Political Economy*, Vol. 78, No. 6, pp. 1292–309 (November/December).

Cramer, J. S. (1958) 'Ownership Elasticities of Durable Consumer Goods', *Review of Economic Studies*, Vol. 25, pp. 87–96 (February).

Cripps, F. and Godley, W. (1978) *The Planning of Telecommunications in the UK*, Cambridge: University of Cambridge, Department of Applied Economics (February).

Cunningham, J. and Jaffee, J. (1975) 'Insight into RAM Costs Aids Memory System Design', *Electronics*, Vol. 48, No. 7, pp. 101–3 (11 December).

Dasgupta, P. (1982) 'The Theory of Technological Competition', London School of Economics: International Centre for Economics and Related Disciplines, Theoretical Economics Discussion Paper 82/46.

Davidson, J. E. H., Hendry, D. F., Srba, F. and Yeo, S. (1978) 'Econometric Modelling of the Time-Series Relationship Between Consumers' Expenditure and Income in the United Kingdom', *Economic Journal*, Vol. 88, pp. 661–92 (December).

Davies S. (1979) *The Diffusion of Process Innovations*, Cambridge: Cambridge University Press.

Deaton, A. S. and Muellbauer, J. (1980) 'An Almost Ideal Demand System', *American Economic Review*, Vol. 70, No. 3, pp. 312–26.

Debreu G. (1959) *Theory of Value, Cowles Foundation Monograph*, 6th Printing (1975), New Haven: Yale University Press.

Derksen, J. B. D. and Rombouts, A. (1937) 'The Demand for Bicycles in the Netherlands', *Econometrica*, Vol. 5, pp. 295–300.

Devletoglou, N. E. (1965) 'A Dissenting View of Duopoly and Spatial Competition', *Economica*, Vol. 32, No. 2, pp. 140–60 (May).

Diewert, W. E. (1974) 'Intertemporal Consumer Theory and the Demand for Durables', *Econometrica*, Vol. 42, No. 3, pp. 497–516 (May).

Dorfman, R. and Steiner, P. O. (1954) 'Optimal Advertising and Optimal Quality', *American Economic Review*, Vol. 44, No. 5, pp. 826–36 (December).

Dummer, G. W. A. (1978) *Electronic Inventions and Discoveries*, 2nd Edition Oxford: Pergamon Press.

Eaton, B. C. (1972) 'Spatial Competition Revisited', *Canadian Journal of Economics*, Vol. 5, No. 2, pp. 268–77 (May).

Eaton, B. C. and Lipsey, R. G. (1975) 'The Principle of Minimum Differentiation Reconsidered: Some New Developments in the Theory of Spatial Competition', *Review of Economic Studies*, Vol. 42, No. 1, pp. 27–49 (January).

Economist, various issues.

EDN (*Electrical Design News*), various issues.

Electronics, various issues.

Electronics Industry, various issues.

Electronics Industry Association (EIA), *Electronics Market Data Book*, various years.

Falk, H. (1977) '"Chipping in" to Digital Telephones', *IEEE Spectrum*, Vol. 14, No. 2, pp. 42–6 (February).

Farrell, M. J. (1957) 'The Measurement of Productive Efficiency', *Journal of the Royal Statistical Society* (Series A), Vol. 120, No. 3, pp. 253–81.

Feller, W. (1968) *An Introduction to Probability Theory and Its Applications*, Volume I, 3rd Edition, New York: John Wiley and Sons.

Fisher, F. M. and Shell, K. (1968) 'Taste and Quality Changes in the Pure Theory of the True Cost of Living Index', in Wolfe, J. N. (ed.), *Value, Capital and Growth*, Edinburgh: Edinburgh University Press.

Folberth, O. G. and Bleher, J. H. (1979) 'The Fundamental Limitations of Digital Semiconductor Technology', *Microelectronics Journal*, Vol. 9, No. 4 (March/April).

Freeman, C. (1982) *The Economics of Industrial Innovation*, 2nd Edition, London: Frances Pinter Publishers.

Frisch, R. (1934) *Statistical Confluence Analysis by Means of Complete Regression Systems*, Oslo: University of Oslo, Economics Institute Publication No. 5.

Gannon, C. A. (1973) 'Central Concentration in Simple Spatial Duopoly: Some Behavioural and Functional Conditions', *Journal of Regional Science*, Vol. 13, No. 3, pp. 357–75 (December).

Gavish, B., Horsky, D. and Srikanth, K. (1983) 'An Approach to Optimal Positioning of a New Product', *Management Science*, Vol. 29, No. 11, pp. 1277–97 (November).

Gorman, W. M. (1956) 'A Possible Procedure for Analysing Quality Differentials in the Egg Market', Iowa Agricultural Experiment Station, Journal Paper J-3129 (November), reprinted in *Review of Economic Studies*, Vo.47, No. 5, pp. 843–56 (October 1980).

Gorman, W. M. (1968) 'The Structure of Utility Functions', *Review of Economics Studies*, Vol. 35, No. 4, pp. 367–90.

Gorman, W. M. (1976) 'Tricks with Utility Functions', in Artis, M. and Nobay, A. R. (eds), *Essays in Economic Analysis*, Cambridge: Cambridge University Press.

Graitson, D. (1982) 'Spatial Competition à la Hotelling: A Selective Survey', *Journal of Industrial Economics*, Vol. 31, No. 1/2, pp. 13–25 (September/December).

Griliches, Z. (1971) (ed.) *Price Indices and Quality Change*, Cambridge, Mass.:Harvard University Press.

Hauser, J. R. and Gaskin, S. P. (1984) 'Application of the "Defender" Model', *Marketing Science*, Vol. 3, No. 4, pp. 327–51 (fall).

Hay, D. A. (1976) 'Sequential Entry and Entry Deterring Strategies in Spatial Competition', *Oxford Economic Papers*, Vol. 28, No. 2, pp. 240–57 (July).

Hoenissen, B. and Mead, C. A. (1972) 'Fundamental Limitations in Microelectronics, I:MOS, II:Bipolar', *Solid State Electronics*, Vol. 15, No. 7 (July) and Vol. 15, No. 8 (August).

Hollingdale, S. H. and Tootill, G. C. (1970) *Electronic Computers*, Harmondsworth, Middlesex: Penguin Books.

Horsley, A. (1983) 'Marshall's Consumer and Quality Choice', London School of Economics: International Centre for Economics and Related Disciplines, Theoretical Economics Discussion Paper 83/81.

Horsley, A. and Swann, G. M. P. (1983) 'A Time Series of Computer Price Functions', *Oxford Bulletin of Economics and Statistics*, Vol. 45, No. 4, pp. 339–56 (November).

Hotelling, H. (1929) 'Stability in Competition', *Economic Journal*, Vol. 39, pp. 41–57 (March).

Houthhakker, H. S. (1952/3) 'Compensated Changes in Quantities Consumed', *Review of Economic Studies*, Vol. 19, No. 3, pp. 155–64.

Ide, T. R. (1982) 'The Technology', in (Chapter 2) Friedrichs, G. and Schaff, A. (eds), *Microelectronics and Society: For Better or Worse*, Oxford: Pergamon Press.

Institution of Electrical Engineers (1979), 2nd International Conference on Automotive Electronics, London.

Ironmonger, D. S. (1972) *New Commodities and Consumer Behaviour*, Cambridge: Cambridge University Press.

Kakamura W. A., and Srivastava, R. K. (1984) 'Predicting Choice Shares under Conditions of Brand Interdependence', *Journal of Marketing Research*, Vol. 21, No. 4, pp. 420–34 (November).

Kamien, M. I. and Schwartz, N. L. (1982) *Market Structure and Innovation*, Cambridge: Cambridge University Press.

Keyfitz, R. (1981) 'A Selective Survey of Spatial Economic Theory', unpublished paper, London School of Economics (April).

Knight, K. E. (1966) 'Changes in Computer Performance', *Datamation*, Vol. 12, No. 9, pp. 40–54 (September).

Kotov, A. V. (1968) 'The Development of Electronic and Quasi-Electronic Telephone Systems', *Telecommunication Journal*, Vol. 35, No. 9, pp. 455–62.

Lambin, J-J. (1976) *Advertising, Competition and Market Conduct in Oligopoly Over Time*, Amsterdam: North Holland.

Lancaster, K. J. (1966) 'A New Approach to Consumer Theory', *Journal of Political Economy*, Vol. 74, No. 2, pp. 132–57 (April).

Lancaster, K. J. (1971) *Consumer Demand: A New Approach*, New York: Columbia University Press.

Lancaster, K. J. (1979) *Variety, Equity and Efficiency*, Oxford: Basil Blackwell.

Lerner, A. and Singer, H. (1937) 'Some Notes on Duopoly and Spatial Competition', *Journal of Political Economy*, Vol. 45, No. 2, pp. 145–86 (April).

Lund, R. T., Sirbu, M. A., Utterback, J. M. *et al.* (1980) *Microprocessor Applications: Cases and Observations*, Report for the Department of Industry, London: HMSO.

McDermott, J. (1978) 'Microprocessor and Microcomputer-Based Control Systems Cut Engine Pollution', *Electronic Design*, Vol. 26, No. 15, pp. 20–6 (19 July).

McWhorter, E. W. (1976) 'The Small Electronic Calculator', *Scientific American*, Vol. 234, No. 3, pp. 88–98 (March).

Marshall, A. (1966) *Principles of Economics*, 8th Edition, London: Macmillan.

Mayo, J. S. (1977) 'The Role of Microelectronics in Communication', *Scientific American*, Vol. 237, No. 3, pp. 192–209 (September).

Mead, C. A. and Conway, L. (1980) *Introduction to Very Large Scale Integration Systems*, Reading, Mass.: Addison Wesley.

Meindl J. D. (1977) 'Microelectronic Circuit Elements', *Scientific American*, Vol. 237, No. 3, pp. 70–81 (September).

Microprocessors and Microsystems, various issues.

Mood, A. M., Graybill, F. A. and Boes, D. C. (1974) *Introduction to the Theory of Statistics*, 3rd Edition, New York: McGraw–Hill.

Mowery, D. C. and Rosenberg, N. (1979) 'The Influence of Market Demand upon Innovation: A Critical Review of Some Recent Empirical Studies', *Research Policy*, Vol. 8, pp. 105–53 (April); reprinted in Rosenberg (1982).

Muellbauer, J. (1974) 'Household Production Theory, Quality and the Hedonic Technique', *American Economic Review*, Vol. 64, No. 5, pp. 977–94 (December).

Nelson, R. L. (1958) *The Selection of Retail Locations*, New York: F. W. Dodge.

New Scientist, various issues.

Northcott, J., with Marti, J. and Zeilinger, A. (1980) *Microprocessors in Manufactured Products*, London: Policy Studies Institute, Report No. 590 (November).

Northcott, J., with Rogers, P. (1982) *Microelectronics in Industry: What's Happening in Britain*, London: Policy Studies Institute, Report No. 603 (March).

Noyce, R. N. (1977) 'Microelectronics', *Scientific American*, Vol. 237, No. 3, pp. 62–9 (September).

Noyce, R. N. and Barrett, C. R. (1979) 'The Automobile and the Microcomputer Revolution: Solving the Reliability Problem', *Proceedings of the 2nd IEE International Conference on Automotive Electronics*, London: Institution of Electrical Engineers (October/November).

Oldham, W. G. (1977) 'The Fabrication of Microelectronic Circuits', *Scientific American*, Vol. 237, No. 3, pp. 110–28 (September).

Osborne, A. and Kane, J. (1981) *4- and 8-Bit Microprocessor Handbook* and *16-Bit Microprocessor Handbook*, Berkeley, California: Osborne and Associates/McGraw Hill.

Penney, B. K. (1977) 'The Implications of Microprocessor Architecture on Speed, Programming and Memory Size', paper presented to the IERE Conference (No. 36) on Computer Systems and Technology, London: Institution of Electrical and Radio Engineers (March).

Petritz, R. L. (1978) 'Technology of Integrated Circuits: Past, Present and Future', *Microelectronics Journal*, Vol. 9, No. 1, pp. 27–36 (September).

Post Office Electrical Engineers Journal (*POEEJ*), various issues.

Power, E. (1941) *The Medieval Wool Trade*, Oxford: Oxford University Press.

Rosen, S. (1974) 'Hedonic Prices and Implicit Markets: Product Differentiation in Pure Competition', *Journal of Political Economy*, Vol. 82, No. 1, pp. 34–55 (January/February).

Rosenberg, N. (1982) *Inside the Black Box: Technology and Economics*, Cambridge: Cambridge University Press.

Rothschild, R. (1976) 'A Note on the Effect of Sequential Entry on Choice of Location', *Journal of Industrial Economics*, Vol. 24, No. 4, pp. 313–320 (June).

Scar, R. W. A. and Swindle, R. I. (1978) 'The Remote Line-Tester', IERE Conference on Microprocessors in Automation and Communication, London: Institution of Electrical and Radio Engineers (September).

Scherer, F. M. (1979) 'The Welfare Economics of Product Variety: An Application to the Ready to Eat Breakfast Cereal Industry', *Journal of Industrial Economics*, Vol. 28, No. 2, pp. 113–34 (December).

Schmalensee, R. (1972) *The Economics of Advertising*, Amsterdam: North Holland.

Schmalensee, R. (1978) 'Entry Deterrence in the Ready to Eat Breakfast Cereal Industry', *Bell Journal of Economics*, Vol. 9, No. 2, pp. 305–27 (autumn).

Schmidt, P. (1976) 'On the Statistical Estimation of Parametric Frontier Production Functions', *Review of Economics and Statistics*, Vol. 58, No. 2, pp. 238–9 (May).

Sciberras, E. (1977) *Multinational Electronics Companies*, Greenwich, Connecticut: JAI Press.

Shaked, A. (1975) 'Non-Existence of Equilibrium for the Two-Dimensional Three Firms Location Problem', *Review of Economic Studies*, Vol. 42, No. 1, pp. 51–6 (January).

Shaw, R. W. (1982a) 'Product Proliferation in Characteristics Space: The UK Fertilizer Industry', *Journal of Industrial Economics*, Vol. 31, No. 1/2, pp. 69–91 (September/December).

Shaw, R. W. (1982b) 'Product Strategy and Size of Firm in the UK Fertilizer Market', *Managerial and Decision Economics*, Vol. 3, No. 4, pp. 233–43 (December).

Smithies, A. (1941) 'Optimum Location in Spatial Competition', *Journal of Political Economy*, Vol. 49, No. 3, pp. 423–39 (June).

Stahl, K. and Varaiya, P. (1978) 'Economics of Information: Examples in Location and Land-Use', *Regional Science and Urban Economics*, Vol. 8, No. 1, pp. 43–56 (February).

Stoneman, P. L. (1976) *Technological Diffusion and the Computer Revolution: The UK Experience*, Cambridge: Cambridge University Press.

Stoneman, P. L. (1983) *The Economic Analysis of Technological Change*, Oxford: Oxford University Press.

Sutherland, I. E. and Mead, C. A. (1977) 'Microelectronics and Computer Science', *Scientific American*, Vol. 237, No. 3, pp. 210–28 (September).

Swann, G. M. P. (1982) 'Multicollinearity and Measurement Error', unpublished paper, London School of Economics (July).

Swann, G. M. P. (1983) 'Quality Improvements in Microcomputer Software: An Introduction', unpublished paper, London School of Economics (July).

Swann, G. M. P. (1984) *The Measurement of Product Competitiveness in Clusters of Similar Products: The Case of Microcomputers*, Report to the Brunel Research Initiative and Enterprise Fund (August).

Swann G. M. P. (1985a) 'Product Competition in Microprocessors', *Journal of Industrial Economics*, Vol. 34, No. 1, pp. 33–53 (September).

Swann G. M. P. (1985b) 'The Measurement of Product Competitiveness with Diverse Consumer Tastes', paper accepted for the Fifth World Congress of the Econometric Society (August).

Swann G. M. P. (1985c) 'International Differences in Product Design and their Economic Significance', discussion paper, Centre for European Industrial Studies, University of Bath (May).

Swann G. M. P. (1985d) *Quality Innovation and Demand: A Study of Microelectronics*, Ph. D. thesis, University of London (February).

Telecommunications Journal, various issues.

Theil, H. (1952/3) 'Qualities, Prices and Budget Enquiries', *Review of Economic Studies*, Vol. 19, No. 3, pp. 129–47.

Theil, H. (1965) 'The Information Approach to Demand Analysis', *Econometrica*, Vol. 33, No. 1, pp. 67–87 (January).

Tilton, J. E. (1971) *International Diffusion of Technology: The Case of Semiconductors*, Washington DC: Brookings.

Triplett, J. E. (1975) 'Consumer Demand and Characteristics', in Terleckyj, N. (ed.), *Household Production and Consumption*, New York: National Bureau of Economic Research.

US Department of Commerce (1975), *Impact of Electronics on the US Calculator Industry*, Washington DC: Government Printing Office (November).

Valery, N. (1975) 'The Electronic Slide Rule Comes of Age', *New Scientist*, Vol. 65, pp. 506–11 (27 February).

Verhofstadt, P. W.J. (1976) 'Evolution of Technology Options for LSI Processing Elements', *Proceedings of the IEEE*, Vol. 64, No. 6, pp. 842–51 (June).

Waugh, F. V. (1929) *Quality as a Determinant of Vegetable Prices*, New York: Columbia University Press.

Webber, M. J. (1972) *Impact of Uncertainty on Location*, Cambridge, Mass.: MIT Press.

Webbink, D. W. (1977) *The Semiconductor Industry: A Survey of Structure, Conduct and Performance*, Staff Report to the US Federal Trade Commission, Washington DC: Government Printing Office (January).

Weber, A. (1929) *Theory of the Location of Industry*, translated by Friedrich, C. J., Chicago: University of Chicago Press.

White, H. (1980) 'A Heteroskedasticity-Consistent Covariance Matrix Estimator and a Direct Test for Heteroskedasticity', *Econometrica*, Vol. 48, No. 4, pp. 817–38 (May).

Whitney, T. M. and Paluck, R. J. (1972) 'MOS Circuit Development for the HP-35', paper presented to the 6th Annual IEEE Computer Society Conference, San Francisco (September).

Whitworth, I. (1980) 'Developments in 16 bit Microprocessors', *Microprocessors and Microsystems*, Vol. 4, No. 1, pp. 17–22 (January/February).

Wills, H. (1978) 'Estimation of a Vintage Capital Model for Electricity Generating', *Review of Economic Studies*, Vol. 45, No. 3, pp. 495–510 (October).

Wilson, R. W., Ashton, P. K. and Egan, T. P. (1980) *Innovation, Competition and Government Policy in the Semiconductor Industry*, Lexington, Mass.: Lexington Books, D. C. Heath and Co.

Wise, K. D., Chen, K. and Yokely, R. E. (1980) Micros—A Technology Forecast and Assessment to 2000, New York: Wiley Interscience.

Author Index

Subject Index